I AM A TEACHER

A Tribute to America's Teachers

▼

Created and edited by David Marshall Marquis

Photographs and interviews by Robin Sachs

Designed by Tom Hough

Simon and Schuster

New York   London   Toronto   Sydney   Tokyo   Singapore

Simon and Schuster
Simon & Schuster Building
Rockefeller Center
1230 Avenue of the Americas
New York, New York 10020

SIMON AND SCHUSTER and colophon are registered
trademarks of Simon & Schuster, Inc.

Designed by Tom Hough
Manufactured in the United States of America

10 9 8 7 6 5 4 3 2 1

Library of Congress Cataloging-in-Publication Data
Marquis, David Marshall, 1951-
    I am a teacher: a tribute to America's teachers/
    created and edited by David Marshall Marquis:
    photographs and interviews by Robin Sachs.
        p.   cm.
    1. Teachers—United States—Interviews.
    I. Sachs, Robin, 1952-
    II. Title.
LB1775.M4294   1990
371.1′00222′2—dc20   90-40680
                                         CIP

ISBN 0-671-72221-2

The statements made in this book are taken from
tape recorded interviews conducted with each
teacher. These tapes were then transcribed and
edited. Every effort has been made to preserve
accuracy while providing for readability.

for Mayme Porter,
my high school speech teacher
She inspired me to become a teacher.
She taught me how to write and perform.
Without her the I AM A TEACHER project
would not exist.

                                    D. M. M.

for my son Adam
His patience and understanding
throughout this project
have enabled me to meet
a few of the most wonderful
teachers in the world.
I wish he could have
every one of them.

                                    R. S.

Acknowledgments

We first wish to acknowledge Jay Fountain, who was present at the moment of the inception of this book and nurtured the idea from the beginning.

We would like to thank Tom Hough — what a designer. Marian Young, our agent, has championed the project from the moment she first saw the photographs. Diana Navarrete has organized our efforts and has made this project manageable. Peggy Ware has with great diligence transcribed the interviews and processed with care the words of our teachers. Special thanks to Walter Nelson for his patient expertise and advice in producing beautiful prints; to Chris Regas, forever a photographic friend and teacher; and to the invaluable photographic assistance of Roxanne DePugh and Jamie Williams, who made life on the road so much more enjoyable. Much appreciation to Sparrow Frenkel, who can do anything. Bob Bender and Johanna Li have come through time and again.

We thank all the people at BWC Photolabs, especially Kristina and Ron. Also our travel agents at Travel One, Ltd.: Becca, Daniel, April and Robin, who have gone above and beyond the call many times. Thanks to Helen, Pat, Debby and Maria at Figure-Logic Business Equipment. We appreciate the assistance of Delta Airlines, in particular Thom Stone.

Thanks to both the Stern family and Mark Donald. Ruthie Woodward has responded graciously, as always, as have M. L. Nelson, David Haselkorn and Rick Bentley. Thanks to Jack Dirmann, Bob Hoffman and Whitney Fair for their help and hospitality. And special appreciation to Billy B. Joiner, Addison Wilson, III, and Kris Gardner.

We offer a most special thanks to all of those who helped us find and locate the teachers included in this book. These nominators gave of their time, postage, long distance, fax machines, photocopiers and, most of all, their care for and commitment to teachers.

And one final acknowledgment: to all our friends who haven't heard from us for so long while we pursued this labor of love. We'll call, we promise.

D. M. M. and R. S.

It was Christmas, 1973, and I had returned home after my first semester as a junior-high history teacher. The family had gone to the traditional Christmas service, which had just ended. There was time for talk, for visiting. The mother of an old friend approached. We hugged, and I asked about Frank.

"Our Frank has just gotten a promotion at the bank. But we're proud of you, too, even if you are just a schoolteacher." She never even knew she had insulted me.

Since that day — that moment — I've had a fire in my gut over the way teachers are treated in this country.

Since May, 1981, my one-person stage show, I AM A TEACHER, has traveled the country making a statement about the importance of teachers. It is based upon my years in the classroom. I've performed it everywhere from school gymnasiums to the Kennedy Center. And yet I have continued to search for other ways to bring recognition to teachers; hence, this book.

When the idea for such a book first came to me, I called Robin Sachs, an old friend and great photographer, because I knew she had what it would take to fulfill the vision of the book, namely, photographic talent and a fiery commitment. Robin knows as I do what the classroom is all about. She spent six years of her life teaching high school English and journalism. In fact, she discovered her gift for photography when she had to teach her kids to take pictures for the school newspaper.

And so we set out to create a book that would be a fitting tribute to teachers, that would once and for all let America's teachers speak for themselves. There have been plenty of books written about teachers, but this book, except for this preface and the brief appendix, comes from the teachers.

These teachers were chosen through a process of plain old-fashioned homework. State departments of education, individual school districts, journalists, teacher associations and educational organizations, superintendents — the list goes on — were all contacted regarding nominations for the book. We sought out every kind of teacher in every imaginable teaching situation representing a wide range of teaching styles and philosophies. Every single state, plus the District of Columbia, is represented here, some more than once.

We did not simply seek out the teachers of the year from various states and districts. While some are represented by their current or former teachers of the year, we are happy to present many unsung heroes as well.

We do not claim that the 78 teachers included in these 70 photographs are the best teachers in the country. But we do feel that they represent what is best about the teaching profession. Perhaps our greatest sadness in the making of this book was that so many wonderful teachers had to be left out for simple lack of space.

Whether the teachers come from Bald Knob, Arkansas, or Brooklyn, New York, they clearly live out and speak of certain basic themes, no matter how divergent their views might be on other topics. We found several common threads running throughout virtually all these interviews. Two especially deserve mention.

First, for good teachers, knowledge of the subject matter is a given. In these recent years of educational crisis, the academic abilities of America's teachers has at times been called into question. But because good teachers do know their subject areas and continue to pursue knowledge throughout their careers, they simply don't talk much about it. Of course we know it, they seemed to be saying. How else could we teach it?

Second, and this can only be stated plainly, is love. A love of learning, a love of teaching, a love of kids. These teachers did not simply talk about "enjoying children" or "caring about kids." Their commitment to their students and to their profession is much deeper and more profound than that. Some used the word love directly. Some found other ways to state it. But a review of our work brought this theme home to us with unmistakable clarity.

Certain of our purpose, we made a commitment to excellence, to do this right. And yet as Robin traveled from Miami, Florida, to Nome, Alaska, and from Los Angeles, California, to Turner, Maine, and as I spent months with the telephone glued to my ear, we redoubled our commitment because of the motivation and even inspiration that we received from the teachers we talked to. In the end, this book represents some 2,569 long distance telephone calls; 5,472 individual exposures of film; 131,266 miles flown and 9,469 miles driven; and over 2,800 pages of interview transcripts.

Anything less and this book would have been unworthy of its subjects.

One final note. Certainly we want teachers to read this book. In fact, in a perfect world, no teacher would have to buy this book. Each would be given one. But perhaps more important than teachers reading the book is the need for parents to read this book. And politicians, too, as well as taxpayers and business and community leaders.

Listen to the teachers. They are speaking for themselves. They are not "just" schoolteachers.

David Marshall Marquis and Robin Sachs
June 5, 1990

I Am a Teacher

A Tribute to America's Teachers

GLORIA ANDERSON

Ms. Anderson is pictured with her daughter
Carla, who is also a teacher.

First grade
Sontag Elementary School
Sontag Community, Virginia

This is what it's all about. If a child can come
to school and feel that you are there not
just to do a job, but because you want to
be . . . because you care . . . they have to take
something away.

LINDA K. HILLESTAD

Geography, sixth grade
Brookings Middle School
Brookings, South Dakota

There's so much negative publicity about teachers.

We're constantly justifying what we are doing in the classroom. We're on the defensive . . . always on the defensive.

"Well, [teachers] aren't doing this, they aren't doing that."

[We] have to show them that we are. Right here. Come to my classroom and see for yourself. There are neat things happening here. The kids are learning. Those aren't the kinds of stories that make the headlines. That just makes me grit my teeth. Just irritates me. The good things don't get the notoriety they should.

JAIME ESCALANTE

Mr. Escalante's teaching inspired the film Stand and Deliver.

Math/AP Calculus (AP is the abbreviation for Advanced Placement courses.)
Garfield High School
Los Angeles, California

I convey passion with the subject I teach. With that I capture the mind of the student.

I make them believe in themselves.

REED ADLER

Mr. Adler teaches fifteen students in a one-room schoolhouse.

Kindergarten through eighth grade
Eagle Creek School
Forty-three miles from Clifton, Arizona

You have to not mind being out away from town, away from telephones. We have no telephones here. We generate our own electricity, pump our own water. You have to be pretty self-sufficient. . . .

It'd be nice to have a secretary.

MARGARET BROWN

Ms. Brown teaches at an alternative school for pregnant high school girls.

J. B. Harville School Away From School
Shreveport, Louisiana

I had a student who, when she first came into our program, was very unconventional. She did not knock on the door. She kicked the door in. We kept her for three years. When she came to us, she could not read or write. Three years ago, she graduated from us.

She came to me one day and said, "Thank you, dear lady. You have given me hope. . . . I'm going to make it just because you have faith in me."

And that was the moment I knew I was going to continue to do this as long as I can. She kicked the door in when she walked in, but she walked out like a lady.

PEGGY ALLAN

Language Arts/Social Studies/Gifted Writing
Greenville Junior High School
Greenville, Illinois

Excellence takes extra time. [If] you're going to give more time to your profession, then of course you are taking time away from other things. The price of excellence is time away from your family, realizing that you probably spend more time with other people's children than your own. Trying to be excellent sometimes takes a toll [on your] health. Sometimes [it] evokes professional jealousy, so there is a price.

My turning point was about six or seven years ago. I think that I was a good teacher, strong in the subject area, got along well with the children, worked very hard. But I wasn't going above and beyond. I was becoming frustrated with the whole system, so I actually had a talk with myself. OK, am I going to stay in this profession or not? And I thought, I have a lot of creative and innovative ideas that I haven't done in the classroom.

Why haven't I done them? The answer was because of the extra time. OK, where can I make up extra time? Instead of going down to the lounge during my break, I could work in my room. We get out of school at 3:30. If I stay 'til 5:30, look at all the planning I could get done. Why couldn't I come up here on Friday night and Sunday afternoon?

So I just told myself, OK, I'm going to give this a shot . . . everything I have. If I don't feel better about it, I'll get out. Then almost immediately, because of course I was much better prepared and much more creative, I started to get so much positive feedback from my students and from their parents. One thing just fed off the other. It was like, how can I top the project that I did last week? It just really changed my whole life. I became an 8:00 to 5:30 teacher, and then weekends. To other people that may be crazy, but I was enjoying it. . . .

Other teachers would say, "I leave at 3:30, and guess what, we get paid the same." And others would say, "Why are you doing this? Nobody cares." It is easy to feel that nobody cares. But I could tell that the kids in my classroom did care. A lot of their parents cared, and some of them told me how much they cared. And in my heart I knew it did matter. I know I am making a difference.

BOBBIE SUE POOLE

Algebra II/Trigonometry/Pre-Calculus/Basic Math/
Department Chair
Southern Nevada Vocational Technical Center
Las Vegas, Nevada

I've had an awful lot of opportunities and
encouragement to go into administration, but
the reason I enjoy going to work is because of
the kids.

Every kid is different. What's exciting is to try
to meet the needs of those individual kids. It is
never boring. It is different from minute to
minute, and there is no formula that works for
everyone.

JIM EISENHARDT

Mr. Eisenhardt now teaches in the same high school
from which he graduated.
Drama/Speech
Omaha South High School
Omaha, Nebraska

I had graduated from high school and really had no money. No car, nothing. I started work [in a] soup factory in downtown Omaha [for] $1.77 an hour . . . I had just planned on working there until I could earn enough money to go to college. But while I was there a woman retired after 44 years of cutting onions. I decided that I couldn't spend 44 years of my life in a factory. Not that it was unworthy of me . . . I don't want to sound like I am saying that being a blue-collar worker is bad. My parents were blue-collar workers . . . It's just

that I needed more. Everything I'd been taught up until that point — all my teachers — I knew there was something more that I could do. So in August I quit work and went to school with $60 in my pocket and worked my way through college.

I was the first high school graduate in my family. I was the first college graduate in my family. It's very important to me. It was very important to them.

So I said I want to go back home where I went to school. I might be able to turn some kids on to realizing that they can come from that community like I came out of the community, and whether they have money or not, go on and make an impact on someone else.

W. DEAN EASTMAN

*Mr. Eastman developed the concept for and
supervised the construction of a simulated
archaeological dig site in his school courtyard.*

*Social Studies
Beverly High School
Beverly, Massachusetts*

We have four different layers here representing
different time elements. We work with the city
archaeologists of Boston. Geologically this is
very accurate. The first layer, we brought in the
archaeology department of Harvard, and they
did Stone Age toolmaking. How you make
arrowheads [or] scrapers, how you harden
tools. Then they put the artifacts they created
in what would look like an exact archaeological
setting. So then we put a layer [of soil]
across that .

Then the next time level would be the
Woodland Era . . . basically Indian ceramic-
making. The city archaeologist came in and
he made a kiln right here and showed the
different types of pottery that were indigenous
to this area.

The next layer on the top of that is a Colonial
one. Brick, stone, ceramics, flatware, clay
pipes. We have a modern layer in there . . .
the idea of ecology. Things that aren't
biodegradable. Diapers, beer cans, pull tabs.
So there's that level.

Everyone's getting involved. The vocational
wing built it. Volunteers brought in the dirt.
The art department made a lot of the ceramics
that we put in down there. The math
department, too, because when you do the
analysis, a lot of it is percentages. Geology.
Geography, for mapping the site.
Interdisciplinary has to be integrated.

Once we dig this stuff up, that's not the end of
it. We have a lab where we can analyze things.
There has to be an analysis. That's where the
critical thinking comes in.

[My] course isn't just the archaeology pit. We
[also] have this video exchange program with
schools from across the country. We're just now
getting started. We made a video of the Boston
Freedom Trail [and] the live reenactment of
the Boston Tea Party. What this whole network
would be, for example, is you call up [a school
in] San Antonio, Texas. "Listen, we have
videos you might be interested in. If you give
us one on the Alamo, we'll give you any one
that we have." So far, we've got about 50
responses.

[Also] we feel we have to write the real history
of Beverly. [Students] are using old census
records, diaries and microfilm to get a better
idea of the contributions of women and
minorities [from] the seventeenth to the
twentieth century . . . We have to get a better
idea of how the average person [lived].

We're starting our video genealogy where
multigenerational families from Beverly can
come in. We're going to tape it, keep part for
our archives, then give them a tape. We're
doing a lot of things to involve the
community . . . So we become our own
historians.

I love to teach . . . the kids love it . . . this is
where I belong.

Setting High Standards

I don't accept anything but their best. They think a lot of times that I'm asking too much. That doesn't mean it has to be perfect . . . what they turn in. But they know if I'm going to give them a good mark, it's going to have to have excellence. I'm a hard taskmaster. They didn't know they could do as well as they could until they tried to meet my challenge.

Bettye McLaughlin
Arkansas

I'm tough as nails. But they know that I love them . . . They don't have to love me, but they have to respect me. And they have to respect themselves. They have to learn something that they can take with them because they can't take me with them, and they can't take mom with them and they can't take the neighbor with them. They can only take what's inside their own head.

Johanna Brown
Michigan

I demand 100 percent, and then I demand 150 percent. And then I demand 200 percent. You cannot satisfy me. Whatever you do, I force you to move on. Part of life is learning how to deal with frustrations. [If] they can't deal with it in a classroom, they're going to have a hard time dealing with it in life, so [they] may as well start now.

I think kids are like faucets. Because when I was teaching college, the same kid would write a horrible piece of junk for another professor, and for me they would just [write] beautiful stuff. Because they know that if they don't, I'm going to give it back and tell them to do it over. And I'm not only going to give it back to them, I'm going to yell at them, scream at them, coax them, cajole them and everything else until they do it right. Then after they do it right, I'll tell them it's not good enough. I want more.

George Guthridge
Alaska

I tell them at the beginning of the year that I have a goal for each of them. That goal is for them to become the best fourth graders in the whole wide world. I'll ask them, "How many of you would like that to happen?" And, of course, they all raise their hands. I say, "OK, I'm going to tell you how that can happen." I go through the spiel about . . . [how] they've got to do their homework. You zap them with all the work they have to do. But after telling them all the work they are going to have to do, I say, "I'm going to help you do all this, folks. You're not doing it alone. I'm going to help you do this. If you stay with me, work with me every day, cooperate, always try your best, have a good attitude, when we finish at the end of the year, you'll be the best student you can be. And if you're the best student you can be, then you're the best student in the world."

Ivan Neal
Delaware

A lot of times we don't expect enough of the students. That to me is lack of respect. To me, *expect* is *respect*. In other words, if you don't expect something of someone, they'll be satisfied with less. I think that's been done with women and minorities throughout the years. And they'll never see that next plateau. So I think you have to make it fairly rigorous. If they don't get it, just sit down and roll up your sleeves and *be* with them. It seems to work.

W. Dean Eastman
Massachusetts

You Have to Pay for That

I think that somehow we teachers have to get the message out to the public that even though we are dedicated and have so much personal pride and commitment and are so conscientious, there [comes] a point. I resent very much when board members present the choice to teachers: "OK, we only have so much money. What do you want next year, a raise or smaller class size?" With the implication being that if you are a true professional, you'll take smaller class size.

I would answer, "I want both." To which I had a board member say to me once, "You want it all." And I thought, what do you mean I want it all? I resent having to make that decision. I want what is good for the children. What is good for my students is a well-qualified professional and smaller class size. You have to pay for that.

Peggy Allan
Illinois

That's the reality of our society. Those things they value, they pay for. Those things they don't value, they don't pay for.

Verleeta Wooten
Washington

It's not just a matter of concern for educators or just a matter of concern for parents whose children are in the classrooms . . . I think that our leaders need to actually show some leadership by putting their money where their mouth is.

Jenlane Gee
California

CHARLENE BICE

Third grade
J. T. Stevens Elementary School
Fort Worth, Texas

One of the highlights of my teaching career was when we integrated for the first time. I had never taught mixed races before. And I realized that all children were the same. It didn't matter what their color was, didn't matter where they were from, or who they were. If I motivated them and challenged them, they would learn.

DOLLY NARANJO

Ms. Naranjo is a Native American of the Santa Clara Pueblo.

Kindergarten teacher/Principal
Tesuque Pueblo Day School
Tesuque Pueblo, New Mexico

I work here for three-year time periods, then I take a year off. . . Mostly because I feel that I give 150 percent when I'm working, and I don't have the ability not to. I've tried to modify that, maybe being a little more temperate with how much I do and how much I give. I can't do that.

One of the worst things I could think of would be to burn out and not ever want to teach again, so the system I have keeps me from doing that.

I'm a potter, as well. I pot all the time. When I'm teaching, I'll save all my pot money so that when I'm not teaching I can live on that.

JACQUELINE MILES STANLEY

Ms. Stanley has taken a leave of absence from her middle school classroom to become a Teacher in Residence at the South Carolina Center for Teacher Recruitment.

Ohorry County, South Carolina

My responsibilities . . . are in the areas of minority recruitment . . . to expand the pool for possible minority teachers. . . .

I think everybody needs to understand that teachers come in all shapes and sizes and all colors and that they should be appreciated for what they bring to the profession, not where they came from. . . .

I enjoy the work I do for the center because in the long run I know that many more children will benefit. But I miss that closeness. I miss those smiles. I do, I miss those children.

PAMELA ADAMS JOHNSON

Science/Sixth grade
Carpenter Elementary School
Monticello, Iowa

What makes a good teacher a great teacher
is that they pick up on those unexpected
things a student will bring in. I had a student
bring in eyeballs from a cow! So you sort of
say . . . "Well, this is what the students are
interested in today."

Let's do something unexpected.

They're interested in it and so am I . . . let's
go with it. That's what you do in teaching.
You know when it's time to be flexible.

RONALD G. SUVAK, Sr.

American History/Coach
West Woodland Hills
Junior High School
Pittsburgh, Pennsylvania

DOLORES CLOUGHERTY SUVAK

American Literature
Woodland Hills High School
Pittsburgh, Pennsylvania

RONALD: A quarter to six, we are up and at 'em. I'm usually out the door at 6:15.

DOLORES: Our little one doesn't have to start school until 8:15. Drop him at Grandma's one block away. My brother drops him at his school two blocks away. It's a real family affair.

The high school starts at 7:15. My school doesn't start 'til 8:00. But I'm there by 6:30, getting lessons ready, running things off, whatever.

We pack lunch the night before . . . That saves a few minutes.

She's done at 2:30, then starts her cheerleading activities. I'm either at football practice or basketball practice.

If I'm making dinner, I get it started, then do lesson plans.

We usually meet up here at 5:30.

Our lives intertwine so much.

We either [go to] high school football or basketball games. Or down to see our other son at Carnegie-Mellon.

We're not out every evening, by any means.

Just three nights a week.

I couldn't be the teacher I am without having his support, knowing what it's like in the classroom.

Every day is something new. Meeting new people . . . all the activities.

And it just becomes — it's fun. It's *fun*. It's being there. I keep looking at myself and saying, "You're 41, not 16." . . . Twenty years I've gone to proms. We still chaperone the prom.

We must hold the record in that. There's some times we would rather stay home, but . . . seeing these kids as eighth graders, worrying about who their next boyfriend or girlfriend is going to be. And then you see them at the senior prom. For me that's a good feeling . . . to see that they've grown and matured.

We met in college, taking the same education course. We started our career in the same school.

We do have good conversations around the table . . . the commonality of discussing the day. Never a dull moment.

We are off in the summer together.

That's true.

That's when I dust.

JANICE HERBRANSON

Teacher/Principal/Cook/Janitor
Kindergarten through sixth grade
Salund School
McLeod, North Dakota

This is home. I grew up in the country and
went to a country school for eight years. Then
I went to a city high school and college.
I believe in the country school. If I didn't
believe that it was a good education,
I wouldn't be here. The one-to-one
teaching . . . is important. You don't have so
many get lost in the shuffle. When there's a
problem, you can catch it right away.

I'm surprised some people think just because
it's big it's good. That isn't necessarily so.

CLEMONTENE W. ROUNTREE

General Science/Biology
Alice Deal Junior High School
Washington, D.C.

Science frightens them, and it should not. All
in all, the children have been told so long that
you can't do [science], that it's only for an elect
group. Which isn't true... We have to have an
intelligent community of people that can make
everyday decisions on pollution, on whether
they want the dump next door to them.
Or what this chemical plant is doing to my
water... We're going to have to take the fear
out of it. [Science] is right in front of us.
In every classroom, in every building and
at home.

SISTER PAULINE LEMAIRE

Preschool
Providence Montessori School
Portland, Oregon

Children have a right to grow into the persons
they were meant to be and not some common
denominator. They have a right to explore their
interests. When a child is ready to walk, they
do it. You can't hold them down. I think
intellectually it is the same thing. . . .

Montessori comes the closest . . . [to] what I
believe the dignity of the human person is.

BOB SCHROEDER

Fourth grade
Swasey Central School
Brentwood, New Hampshire

There's no doubt. Learning is like breathing.
Learning is natural. People are born to it.
People aspire to it.

Learning is what we are.

LYNN M. MACAL

The Tesseract School is operated as a for-profit business by Education Alternatives, Inc. Stimulated by educational research funded initially by a major corporation, a group of individuals turned the concept of the school into a reality by obtaining private funding from investors. Education Alternatives, Inc., also operates a school in Phoenix, Arizona.

First grade
Tesseract School
Eagan, Minnesota

The term "tesseract" actually means another dimension.

I really don't know how to describe being a teacher here. [At] this school teachers, above and beyond anything else, share a feeling of love and caring toward the students.

[Tesseract] doesn't cater to specific children with specific IQ's. No one takes special tests to get into our school. Children come here for a lot of different reasons . . . The dream is that this is a school that is good for every child. What works for one will never work for another. Everything works and everything doesn't work. We all have different modes of learning. We try to interrelate or interlock as many things as we can. How will math figure in? Is social studies a part [of this]? Science needs to be [included]. Are we going to teach reading through this? We use everything that we can get our hands on . . . a real melting pot of textbooks and curriculum and a wonderful opportunity to do what the children feel they need.

We do test. It's very difficult to measure. We test for their sakes really because they will be tested in their life. So we try to find the best way to test them. We do give a standardized test at the beginning of the year and at the end of the year. It carries whatever weight it needs to carry. We don't center our curriculum

around it . . . It gives us some information. It says work on this. Give as many opportunities as you can for this child in this area.

Each of our master teachers has an associate teacher. It's vital for us. Kelly Vogel is my associate teacher. She helps with teaching all the areas of the curriculum. If I didn't have Kelly, it would be much more difficult to do individualization. Kelly had a degree in business [but] . . . felt that her true calling was education. So she went back to school and got her degree in elementary education.

All of our associate teachers are certified teachers. They could have a job anyplace else. But they appreciate the philosophy of the school.

Every child has a gift and a talent. We accept the responsibility to find and nurture that. I would hope that they would leave first grade thinking, there isn't anything I can't do. Kind of a hunger to do, to be, to try.

Think of how much more they have to give if we just ask the right questions.

Learning Should Be

If you can't laugh at yourself, you might as well hang it up. And you've got to laugh with the students, too. There are some teachers who think that it's against the law for you to smile or to laugh in class. Oh! You won't have any control then. But sometimes kids just do the silliest things. It's laughable, so you do. . .

I just plain have fun. I am totally unpredictable. You might come in here sometime when I'm up on top of a desk doing something. . . .

I guess teaching allows you to be creative. It's never routine. It's never boring. My mind is always going. And I like learning. I learn an awful lot as I'm helping my kids learn. I think that's one of the best examples I can set for them. Wow, I didn't know that! Hey, look at this! Teachers don't know everything. We're still learning all the time.

Linda K. Hillestad
South Dakota

Kids are very unpretentious about their boredom. If we aren't doing, we aren't really learning and having the kind of fun we can have with learning. I value fun a great deal. If I am not having fun, I am not going to be here. And I can't talk all the time and have fun. I like to see the kids have fun, and I like to see myself have fun. Doing has a lot to do with that.

Bob Schroeder
New Hampshire

Learning should be fun. I feel like they learn so much more. It's just a matter of wanting to learn and being involved. They ask much better questions. I just feel like they go out with an attitude of questioning and excitement and wanting to learn more and knowing ways to learn.

Richard Spry
Tennessee

At the end of the week I always look back and say, "What did we accomplish this week? What did I want to accomplish? Was it a good week? Did we have fun learning?"

Bill Collar
Wisconsin

Isolation and Support

It's important to increase people's morale and let them know that there is a support system out there. Because I think we're losing some of our best and brightest when we don't give them the encouragement that they need. Teaching is very isolated... We're so busy all day, we may not see each other until the very end. There's no time. You're getting ready for the next moment, dealing with scraped knees. Dealing with a problem, a parent calls you, paperwork to be done. Being there for teachers is a key to a successful school... teachers working together and feeling good being there. Because they know there's some sort of safety net out there where someone's going to take the time for them.

Jenlane Gee
California

A lot of us do [isolate ourselves] because we say we only have time to go in there and do the classes. But three minutes, four minutes out of your day, you can just talk to another teacher.

Gail McCready Staggers
Connecticut

I tell [first-year teachers], "Never think that you are out there by yourself." Don't be afraid to say, "Help me, I need help." Sometimes we want to be the best teachers. Especially the first year, we want to say, "I know this is what's going on and I don't need any help." But we all need help. So I tell my interns, "Don't be afraid to say, 'Help me.'" And I tell them to always make friends with everybody — the front office, the custodians, cafeteria staff, librarians, everybody — because you're going to need them. In a school, you're working with the young people, and everybody needs everybody else.

Ernestine Hogan
Georgia

Teachers supporting teachers. Or colleagues supporting colleagues. Go away from the emphasis on the problem and come back to the emphasis on teaching. I care about you and you care about me. Why? Because we are teachers. We are special people, and I think that's important. We're not separate. We just teach in different systems. But the aim is the same. Children. If that aim is for a better world, then it must be the same thing. Care about each other as teachers. Support one another. That's what it's all about.

Yvonne Rhem-Tittle
New York

BARBARA HINES HESTER

Art
Ballard High School
Louisville, Kentucky

When you're talking about someone educated,
you're talking about a well-rounded
person . . . not a bookworm. How on earth
educators, administrators, politicians can talk
to us about leaving art out of the curriculum
and talk about building well-rounded people, I
do not understand. You introduce someone to
me at age 50 who is going to sit down at their
leisure and do a physics problem, and I will
laugh at your story. You tell me someone's
going to an exhibit, going to a concert [or]
picking up a piece of artwork [and] working on
it themselves, there'll be a million of them out
there. It's a part of us. It is a part of our inner
beings. Don't talk to me [about] "just art."

EDWARD J. WONG

American History/AP American History/
Mississippi River History
Vicksburg High School
Vicksburg, Mississippi

I think everybody else gets a kick out of the fact that here I am . . . a Chinese-American teaching American history [in Mississippi]. It's funny to everyone but my kids. I think my kids accept it better than a lot of adults do because of the respect and love that we have for each other.

Kids say that I listen to them. Regardless of color, that comes out. . . I grew up with black children, I went to school with white children. We share the same heritage . . . Black and white southerners share more in common than they have apart is what I'm trying to teach them.

I still live in a very ideal world. As a teacher I still think — call it naive or call it idealistic — that maybe I can make a difference. I don't know whether I can or not, but I haven't given up on thinking that. As long as I think I can, then I'm going to stay in this profession.

THE SIXTH GRADE TEAM

From left to right:
Marilyn Aden, Susan Lloyd, Taeko Horwitz,
Nina Pearson, Debra West, Debi Edwards

Academy for Science and Foreign Language
Huntsville, Alabama

SUSAN LLOYD:

Positive school. Positive. You can tell when
you walk in the front door. The students are
empowered. The teachers have been
empowered also. . . .

If someone has an idea, we try to do it. We
try not to say no. The team tries just about
anything. We really do. It's just that kind of
a thing. If someone says, "Let's try this," . . .
we do.

NINA PEARSON:

Our students have to become much more
independent and much more responsible. So
we asked the parents . . . to quit reminding
them 14 times, "Have you done your
homework yet?" . . . Even if it means the child
actually flunking one six weeks . . . Allow the
child to flunk in math and he would realize,
"Aha! This was *my* problem. *I* was the one who
didn't turn the homework in."

DEBRA WEST:

When you integrate [learning], they see how it
all fits together. It's not just math, it's not just
science, it's not just language arts . . .
Everything fits in the puzzle.

TAEKO HORWITZ:

This is the only school in [the] whole state
of Alabama where Japanese is taught. The
Japanese language is getting more popular. It's
quite in demand.

MARILYN ADEN:

Our knowledge base is growing at such a rapid
rate, it's ridiculous to think they can learn [a]
body of facts. What they need to know is how
to think and where to find those facts when
they need them.

DEBI EDWARDS:

I told [another teacher] that I had a job at the
academy. She said, "Oh, you're going to
work yourself to death. You picked the one
school that they stay 'til dark and they work
all summer."

And I said, "Sounds good to me."

J.J. CONNOLLY

Mr. Connolly has been teaching in the same school for 41 years.

English/Latin/Ancient History
St. Mark's School of Texas
Dallas, Texas

Kids today are as smart as ever. But everything has to be immediate, present, here, now and no waiting. So history. . .takes a backseat. Anything then can be made irrelevant or seem irrelevant because it doesn't fit their present scope. And that's another thing you have to teach them. That they are the product of something, and that they will hopefully be the development of something else.

IVAN NEAL

Fourth grade
Frankford Elementary School
Frankford, Delaware

I know in some cases that I am the father figure
for children. It's obvious from the interaction.
I am it. I try, God knows. . . .

You can't just think you're going to work from
8:00 to 3:00 and go home and that's it.
There's just too much at stake. . . . I wish
I were perfect.

Ms. McEntee and her husband, who is also a teacher, take their boat across Narragansett Bay each morning from the island where they live to the mainland.

English
Toll Gate High School
Warwick, Rhode Island

Everybody's a writer... I used to think you were either a writer or not a writer. That's not the case at all.

When I was a sophomore in high school...I decided to join a creative writing class. But the teacher didn't really think that I was a good writer, and I probably wasn't. But she didn't think I was serious. [That's] what really bothered me so much. So when I left that class I just felt that I wasn't a good writer at all. I didn't think about writing again until I was 36 years old. I decided I would take a writing course in the summer, just a freewheeling kind of thing. I started writing poetry... I kept a journal for seven years, and I published...

Part of it is realizing the struggle. I know if I hadn't become a writer that I would never have made that connection. I can say to all of my students, whatever your first draft is, it's just a draft... So it's a mess. So what? So do another draft. Get a friend to help you.

Three or four drafts down the road you've got a deadline. I'm going to give you a grade on that. But you know what? If you get a chance even a month down the road, take that piece out of your folder and work on it again. Maybe we can send it to some contest or maybe you want to get a little better grade. Let's try it again.

MARJORY MOE

Librarian/Media Specialist
Alpine School
Sparta, New Jersey

With the change now in information technology, most librarians are pedaling very fast to stay with the changes in the computer world and the changes in delivering information to our students . . . In New Jersey we now have a library [computer] network. [Students] are going to be accessing information from all over the world.

But to continue their education, they also need to continue to enjoy reading . . . the sheer enjoyment of reading for reading's sake.

MARK SAUL

Math/Geometry/Computer Coordinator
Bronxville School
Bronxville, Westchester County, New York

What's the beauty of math? Oh, how can I
tell you? How can I begin to tell you?

The Wrong Profession

If teachers aren't given the chance, the status quo will remain. A good teacher would like nothing better than to help a mediocre teacher. And a committed teacher would like to shoot those teachers who leave the building right after school's out and are never seen again until the next morning. When we all agree that teaching is not a nine-to-five job, then we'll understand professionalism. More and more teachers want to be able to say, "OK, you have got to straighten up or get out of teaching." We should be allowed to govern our own. To decide who should and who should not be in the profession. And help those who are in the wrong profession to find a way either to become suitable for the profession or [to find] another.

Jim Eisenhardt
Nebraska

Accountability

I can understand the national move toward accountability. But at the same time I'm bothered by it for several reasons. One is that accountability has the potential to breed mediocrity. I'm fearful that if we get into minimum competencies, we will not [be] pushing students toward their potential. I'm worried that minimum competencies will push teaching and students toward lower standards. I think, too, with the paperwork that's involved in accountability, that it hurts the good teachers. I can understand how it may help the mediocre or below-average teacher, but I think it sorely hurts the good teacher because it bogs them down. It's detrimental to their morale.

Edward J. Wong
Mississippi

I don't think there's anything wrong with accountability. But I'm suspicious of some of the [testing] instruments we are using. A few isolated states are getting away from the standardized multiple-choice testing. They ask for student portfolios, or they go in and actually observe students working in the classroom. I think teachers have been asking for this for a long time. Come in and watch my class. Evaluate their writing rather than whether they can do a standardized test. I think that will keep teachers involved because finally you're getting at the real product of what students are doing. I don't mind having my students evaluated as long as the measurement is valid and reliable.

Pamela Adams Johnson
Iowa

We've got to remember that parents and children also hold responsibility for what goes on inside this building. Teachers can only assume so much responsibility because we only have control over so much. Until teachers can contribute to the budget of the school, to the rules and regulations of the school, to the hiring and firing in the school, until we are empowered to do that, don't hold me accountable. Because I have no way of changing what I have to work with. I can't change the fact that there's no money for the books that I need. If I can't change what's in the home, I can't change the [child] who comes to school. I take my work very seriously, but until those things are corrected, I do not want to hear about people holding me accountable.

Susan Lloyd
Alabama

I don't just take an interest in my own students here. I try to care about all of the kids on the playground. They're my kids. Yeah. Quote this: "They're my kids." But, you know, they're all of our kids. All of the kids are our kids.

Jenlane Gee
California

Editor's note:

What is it that draws a number of excellent teachers to the same school? On the following five pages are four teachers from the same high school: Jackson Hole High School in Jackson, Wyoming. While many schools represented in the book also have more than one outstanding teacher on their faculties, we found this situation to be unique.

MICHELLE PECK

Government/AP Government/Economics
U.S. History/AP U.S. History/World History
Girls' Basketball Coach
Jackson Hole High School
Jackson, Wyoming

Administrators, hey, they make their building either a conducive atmosphere to teaching, or they make it a hostile atmosphere. It can be rough if you don't get along. Mr. Storrs is a great principal.

DAVE MASTERMAN

Science
Jackson Hole High School
Jackson, Wyoming

JOHN HOWARTH

Mr. Howarth is a native of England.
Science
Jackson Hole High School
Jackson, Wyoming

JOHN: I've mounted a little bit of an assault on what I think are low standards. I have taught in four other countries before coming here, and I was so excited and yet so disappointed.

DAVE: It's almost as if the public school system is designed to encourage mediocrity.

American education provides you with the opportunity to be the very best [and] to be the worst.

One student was socially out of it . . . flunking school. He was going to drop out. I just gave him heck . . . wouldn't let him get away with being lazy. He really grew. He graduated with top honors from MIT.

I didn't know if I could match up to people like Dave Masterman, but I knew I was capable. I think the principal had more of an insight. He said, "I really would like to get you working with Dave."

We've designed a lot of ways to use the computers as laboratory tools. It opens up a whole realm of possibilities . . . I wanted to use [computers] in the classroom, so I sat down and wrote a couple of programs. I guess I've been pretty heavily involved in curriculum development. Last I heard about 8,000 teachers are using those first two programs I wrote.

Apart from [needing] more equipment, there's never enough time. I have a policy never to leave until the students have finished. Some days I'm here three hours after school with students. Give me more time.

I think a student who gets both our classes has a very full spectrum of skills that otherwise would be impossible if they just took my classes or just took John's.

Science is important in itself. But it's more important to teach them what they are capable of and let them earn their self-respect.

Most of all, good sound judgment. Making decisions with substance. Science is a great tool to teach some of those kinds of things on the high school level. It gives the students a security and peace of mind to know that life is consistent.

I see so many problems with the kids.

I think the household is not as strong. Nationally speaking a lot of values simply are not being taught.

Everything tends to be very superficial. The whole media, the television and magazines, are geared toward that superficiality.

The very first day of class every year, I tell them to put in their notebooks in big letters and permanent ink, "Do not believe a word I say." I want them to take responsibility for their own thinking.

No teacher ever asks anything unreasonable — no decent teacher. But many ask for things which are way too low. Nobody learns anything by taking the easy route.

I want them to be critical in a positive way.

Challenge is a good thing. I'm constantly arguing with other teachers about that. Too many people see challenge as a chance to fail. Failure is in itself a learning experience. This is how I develop. This is how I learn.

I love what I do. It's a thrill to wake up and be alive.

I barely get through on what I'm paid here, but I get through because of the sheer thrill I can get from trying to incite and challenge people in the classroom.

My personal objective is to know how every one of my students thinks.

There's never anything too difficult.

STEVE GARDINER

English/Journalism
Jackson Hole High School
Jackson, Wyoming

Cowboys on Everest is kind of an interesting nickname. The trip to Everest started as a project [of] the Wyoming Centennial. The Wyoming Centennial Everest Expedition . . . The man who was the expedition leader [said], "Let's provide a scholarship for a teacher." The school district was very much in favor, and my wife and family were supportive. So I spent three months on this expedition in the fall of '88.

As the teacher/scholarship winner I had some specific jobs . . . We had a satellite connection right to our base camp, so I was calling from Mt. Everest with radio reports six days a week, which were then broadcast all over Wyoming. Also, we found some funding to allow me to produce classroom lessons. We had a nutrition expert, [so] I explained high-altitude nutrition. We had a geologist, and I had him explain how the Himalayas were created. We had people doing medical research on high-altitude physiology . . . I was called the Teacher on Everest.

[The lessons] have been passed around to various schools in the state . . . I've done slide shows. Somewhere in the neighborhood of 5,000 students have now seen a one-hour presentation on Everest.

I try to not only show them the factual chronology of the trip, but I talk about goal-setting and pushing yourself beyond limits. Reaching the summit of Everest is an extremely large goal . . . We didn't reach the summit. We established camp five at 25,000 feet, only 4,000 feet from the summit . . . The percentage of people who attain that goal is very small. And yet, because we had that goal, we were able to attain other smaller goals . . . our geological goals, our medical goals. The larger goal gave us the vehicle to produce smaller goals.

I use that with them. You can do difficult things. Things that you think you can't do. It might be a kid who is going to attempt to read a longer book than he has ever read before. Or selling an advertisement for the year book. Or writing a poem in iambic pentameter. Things that they initially think they can't do. And yet they realize, I can do this.

That summit at Everest? I want that to be out there. I may not quite get there. But by moving in that direction it will make me aware of what I want.

I look for opportunities to grow . . . to be really alive. And then I encourage them to do that, too.

MAC WESTMORELAND

Physical Education /Adventure Program
Irmo Middle School
Columbia, South Carolina

I want to be able to cater to the nonathlete and have them feel good about coming. That's where phys-ed has lacked in the past. There's lots of kids that love to come and some that absolutely despise coming. I feel for those that despise coming. I feel for those that strike out at the plate. I don't like to have 'em strike out. I really don't. . . .

This particular program guarantees that they don't strike out 'cause the group looks after them. Everyone's a star sometime in the Adventure Program. Sometimes it's the smartest, sometimes it's the most agile . . . sometimes it's the smallest, sometimes it's the biggest. I wish I knew a way for that to absolutely permeate everything that we're doing from a phys-ed standpoint. The ones that don't normally go home talking about phys-ed, do when they're enrolled in this . . . I like to see 'em all hit a home run.

LORRAINE "SAMMY" CRAWFORD

World History/AP U.S. History
Soldotna High School
Soldotna, Alaska

I love it. It's fun, it's exciting. It's stimulating. It's rewarding.

But teaching as a whole is very, very, very lonely. You're in a classroom alone with a lot of kids, but you don't have much contact with adults. There's rarely an adult that really understands what you're doing. Other teachers rarely come into my classroom, and I don't have time to go to theirs. We're just too busy. In other jobs people see what you do and they understand. But in teaching, you can have everybody do really well on a test [and] nobody knows about it. Or you had a great discussion on the difference between the Romans and Greeks, and you were just absolutely ecstatic. But nobody ever knows about that.

It's a very lonely profession. You're in there every day doing it and having a wonderful time, but [there's] not much recognition. Except that you know you're doing a good job.

GEORGIE MOUTON

French
Lafayette High School
Lafayette, Louisiana

I'm an American, and I'm proud of being an American. But I'm of French-Acadian ancestry, and I should be proud of that, too. It's true we should speak in English. We're Americans, and we do need to speak English. But . . . I feel that they can use another language . . . and broaden themselves. I'm hoping to give them a broader view. A second language . . . will give them a vision to the future.

RUTH JEAN ANDERSEN

Ms. Andersen has been teaching elementary school in the same community for 33 years. She is pictured with one of her current students and a student from her very first class.

First grade
Anthony Elementary School
Anthony, Kansas

There is nothing more important than learning how to read. If you do not know how to read, what else can you do? And one tries not only to teach them to read, but to teach them to enjoy reading. . . .

In first grade, at the first of the year, they can't read sentences, just very simple sentences. And at the end, in May, when you tell them goodbye, they can read books. That is really a big achievement.

CELIA VAIL

Adult Basic Education
Marion Correctional Institute
Marion, Ohio

[My students] are all men . . . incarcerated for a multitude of offenses. The average is 30 to 35 years old. I have two older, some younger.

They are reading below a fifth-grade level . . . Math skills are a little bit higher. But basically their reading is the major problem.

Most of them say, "If I can just read, I could do anything. Just teach me to read."

There are 30,000 inmates in Ohio prisons. Thirty percent cannot read above the sixth-grade level. Seventy-five percent do not have high school diplomas.

I would say that I have never received such reinforcement from any group. Very few high school kids will say, "You're doing a good job." I get that here. I get them responding with, "Yeah, you're doing okay." So I feel very close to a lot of my people.

We do a lot of individual conferencing . . . One person last week said, "You know, it's a shame I had to come to jail to learn that I need an education."

Administrators

Administrators' jobs are very, very demanding. They really are expected to supervise the hockey games and to do all that. But it seems to me that if we really want excellent schools, that we really need to have instructional leaders. People who are helping us in the classroom develop the materials and work with kids and figure out ways to pay more attention to what is supposed to go on in the school. Administrators are so busy. I mean, my principals are working like crazy. They're really very, very, very hard workers and very dedicated. But they're so busy with discipline and with cleaning up in the lunchroom and with taking care of all of the duties that they have, supervising the buses and making sure the building is maintained well. [In] doing all those things, the primary purpose of the school, it seems to me, is lost. The whole climate of the school . . . should be geared toward working with kids and for kids in the curriculum areas.

Lorraine "Sammy" Crawford
Alaska

Our principal is the type of guy I enjoy working with because he realizes my teaching style. He doesn't create all kinds of obstacles for me. He just allows me to do my thing. I think he feels that Collar is dependable, he's reliable. He's conscientious. Let's just kind of stay out of his way. That's my feeling about administrators. When you have outstanding teachers on your staff, the number one thing you can do is just allow them to teach. Allow them to do their thing. I've done a lot of research into learning styles and teaching styles. So often we try to force people to conform to our expectations of them rather than allow them to develop to their full potential. If I was with an administrator who demanded complete, thorough lesson plans that I must follow all the time, a rather concrete sequential type of thinker, I would have a great deal of difficulty. Because I tend to be an intuitive, random, rather abstract [thinker] at times, but I know where I'm going. And that is my strength. So, you just have to allow me to do that.

Bill Collar
Wisconsin

They have to have vision. We have an incredible assistant superintendent here who is the kindest man in the world. He's truly divinely inspired, and always, when you talk to him, *you* were the phone call he was waiting for. In my mind that's the kind of gift that an administrator should have. Except on the other side of the coin, there has to be a firmness there, too. How do you do all of that? You have to be all things to all people. Hard. Hard.

Johanna Brown
Michigan

The principal is really fundamentally important. We've had a string of terrible ones, followed by a string of very good ones. We are in a good cycle. During the time when we had terrible principals, people who had no concern for education at all, this place was an absolute disaster. Now it is good, and good means that people have the freedom to show their expertise. Students, teachers, the principal.

When I was first hired years ago, I would never go to the teachers' lounge because there was nothing but complaining and whining. But now if anybody complains, it's a rare event and everybody will stop and listen, like, Gee, what's the matter? We are the same people in a different administrative setting. When people are allowed to do what they are expert at, it's synergistic. People build and build and build together. They are willing to work. They are willing to think new thoughts. If we don't, our students don't.

Dave Masterman
Wyoming

Let's Face It

Let's face it. Schools are social agencies. We've got to have the resources there to deal with the problems of kids.

Verleeta Wooten
Washington

Every time a social ill occurs, who is looked upon to solve it or to handle it? It's the school. I had a state-level supervisor admit to us in a . . . meeting that the attitude of many politicians is [that] if there's something that needs to be added to the school curriculum, elementary teachers can do it. And it's just thrown in. They don't take into consideration . . . the things that we are already doing, the way our time is already overcommitted. Every time we turn around, something new is added. A state-level committee will decide, or some legislator will decide, that we need to have—for example, AIDS education. They'll just say, "Well, each child needs to have 30 hours a year, and you're going to do it." That kind of thing is crazy . . . not taking into consideration what the teachers already have to deal with and what we already have in place.

Ivan Neal
Delaware

I was involved in a round-table discussion which was teachers, community people, business people. In the course of the conversation, I was telling about one kid that I have at school and saying, you know, this is what I deal with day after day. A fellow from the business community said, "Well, you're there to teach English. You're not there to do that. That's not your job." I really didn't know how to answer him because it is my job. I'm parent, I'm psychologist, I'm social worker.

When I started teaching in 1962, the biggest problem that I faced [was that] the boys started wearing their pants too tight. That was a major issue, believe it or not . . . . Most of the kids that started out in kindergarten together were still together. There were very few mothers who worked. Kids, for the most part, had the same last names as their parents. And now it's absolutely bizarre. The demands on me beyond teaching subject matter are absolutely beyond what the public will comprehend. I guess that's one of the things that bothers me so much. I don't think the general public has an idea what it's like in the classroom today.

Roberta Ford
Colorado

You try to teach very basically the things that you hope the parents would teach . . . don't be cruel, don't waste time, don't steal, don't tell lies . . . the don'ts. These are the very, very basic things. You hope that those ideas are simply an affirmation of what they've learned at home. That isn't necessarily true today.

Teachers are doing a lot of parenting.

J. J. Connolly
Texas

Don't make us a social institution. Let us get back to the job of teaching. I want to be a teacher to teach. There should be social institutions to take care of these other things . . . . You can't teach a hungry child. You can't. They have no motivation for learning if their bellies are growling. That has to be taken care of, too. But that has to be taken care of in something more than the education system. And in something more than the time frame of education.

Dolores Clougherty Suvak
Pennsylvania

BERYL LYNNE MIRVILLE

*Ms. Mirville is pictured with members of the
Future Educators of America chapter at Miami
Senior High School. The Dade County Public
Schools have a Future Educator chapter in virtually
every school in the county, with over 8,000 students
participating in grades two through twelve.*

*Language Arts/Introduction to Teaching
Magnet Program, Center for the Teaching Profession
Miami Senior High School
Miami, Florida*

I am really encouraged [about the teaching
profession], especially having an opportunity
to work in this program . . . around a group of
kids who want to be teachers. They are so
enthusiastic. They always have something new
they want to share, something different that
they want to do. These kids have given me so
much. They have taught me.

TERESA R. de GARCIA

Bilingual Education
University Hill Elementary School
Boulder, Colorado

People don't really understand what bilingual is all about. People think bilingual means [that if] you have another language, you drop it very slowly while you are learning English. That's not bilingual. The word root — bi — is two. You have to learn two... I teach math, science, reading, writing in two languages... You have a bilingual program regardless of the two languages. Chinese and French, you name it, whatever.

Have you seen all the statistics that we have now? That [soon] we're going to have more minorities — put them all together, black, blue, yellow, green, brown, whatever — we're going to have more minorities than majorities... The point is that we all have to become members of the same community. We, the grownups, are going to die, and [the children] are going to have to deal with it. If we don't teach Molly to appreciate who Rico is, or Rico doesn't learn to appreciate who Molly is, they are going to have a harder time than we have right now.

SANDY JERNBERG

Fifth and sixth grades
Chiron Middle School
Minneapolis, Minnesota

[Chiron Middle School] was formed when a group of business people and parents in Minneapolis wanted a new idea for a school. So they offered a payment for the best idea. A teacher and principal had the specific idea for our school.

Chiron has no buildings. We move from site to site once every twelve weeks. People were looking for a way to [establish] a relationship between the school and the community. Space is donated to us . . . The University of Minnesota donated two classrooms at their agriculture campus for our science site. We also have a business/law/government site and a performing/visual arts site.

Right now we have two kinds of teachers in our school, site teachers and home teachers. I'm a home teacher, so I'm with my kids from the time they're in fifth or sixth grade until the end of the eighth grade . . . I'm responsible to know where they are physically, mentally, academically. . . .

Whether it's working is hard to say right now. We do know the attitudes have improved. Most parents have told me their kids have never had a better year. The change is really good for the kids.

And to be able to think for themselves. That [was] one of the hardest things [for] our kids. Their whole routine was gone. They were totally lost because they didn't [just] open up their math book or their reading book. They had to think.

So, it is working. They like to come to school. They come sick. We have to tell them to go home, and they won't. That's exciting. . . .

We all run committees that run the school. The parents, [too]. We're learning how to do things as a team. Site based management takes a lot of time. I don't think we realized that. Anytime we try to make a decision, it just takes us forever because we're not good enough at it yet. We're doing a lot of learning.

We do all of this outside of school. All our staff meetings, everything is outside of school hours, and we are not paid anything extra to do it. We are on the same salary as if I walked into a room and opened the books.

It takes a commitment. [Chiron] could be a lot of teachers' dream. It's not for every teacher.

I love having a say in what's going on. I feel professional . . . We have two things we've never had before: phones on our desks and computers with printers.

It could fall flat on its face without the support [of] the school board. Our school board is behind us.

CLEO CHARGING

*Ms. Charging's Native American name
is Shells Corn.
She is a member of the Mandan-Hidatsa tribes.*

*Math, fourth through sixth grades/Home Room,
sixth grade/Elementary principal
Margaret Breuer Elementary, White Shield School
Fort Berthold Reservation, North Dakota*

Traditionally we have very close ties with grandparents anyway, but the grandparents' calendar [gives the student] an extra bond . . . a sense of who they are.

Our elementary had been putting out a calendar for years. [One year] the students wanted to put their grandparents on the calendar. Month by month, a different set of grandparents. So they bugged their grandparents for pictures and started interviewing them.

They learned things about their grandparents that they didn't know . . . what it was like when [they] were their age . . . their heritage and how proud they can be of these people.

Then they put their information on computer and started rewriting and editing. They love the computer, very uninhibited [with] it. We printed it, put it through the copier, then bound it.

One girl's grandfather passed away a few weeks after she finished her project. When she [had] asked him if she could put him in the calendar, he said, "Good." He didn't elaborate, but he got his meaning across.

ROBERT H. SINCLAIR

Chairman of the English Department
Brooklyn Technical High School
Brooklyn, New York

I think Shakespeare or any poet is really useful in today's world. Because communication arts and communication are the two areas that are never out of style. All of those people who may sit at terminals or may be manipulating machinery do have to eventually communicate what it is they've discovered. And that's where we get back to words, which are our means of communication. Beautiful words. Words that are meaningful and poetic...

[The students] have had an experience with verse that will allow them to understand a little bit more about what they can do.

BART MARANTZ

Jazz Orchestra Teacher
Booker T. Washington High School for the
Visual and Performing Arts
Dallas, Texas

You can get to a point in your life where
you want your art form to carry on. And
the way to have any art form carry on
is through a teacher. That's why I'm in
it. I'm certainly not in it for the money.

PHILIP DAIL

Science/Chemistry
Garner Senior High School
Garner, North Carolina

What I get out of teaching is the strength, the
power, the energy of life. To see the influence,
to see the exchange of emotions, to see the
exchange of success, to see the exchange of
frustration, to be part of that with these young
people during a time when their lives are so
chaotic . . . it's a reward in and of itself that
nothing can ever replace.

JEN NELSON

Ms. Nelson is seen with papier-maché sculptures constructed by fifth graders using only trash bags, tape, paper towels, glue and cans.

Art
Mustang Valley Elementary School
Yukon, Oklahoma

You couldn't do this by yourself. You don't do things like this by yourself. You have to have your administration backing you. You have to have your principal backing something . . . as messy and as different as this is. And then you have to have parents who are willing to pitch in there and let their kids bring things and work on things. So it's the support, I'd say.

DOUGLAS : We don't audition children here. We take all kinds. We do not intend or try to solely turn out musicians. The idea of arts-based education is what we're about. All of the disciplines are related.

> **YVONNE :** As a science teacher, to give you an example... how sound travels through the air. And what happens to the sound when it reaches their ear.

The idea of how music relates to math... counting things out, dividing, proportionalizing. In terms of reading, they're training their eyes to follow. [While] looking at notes on a staff, they're doing a coding process.

> The arts program also teaches discipline. [If] students can sit down and concentrate on a piece of music, they can sit down and really listen to a lesson when I'm teaching.

I think I figured out once [that students] average two music classes every day.

> It's not a separate entity. When concert time comes about, we are all involved, academic and fine arts. We're there in support of one another.

Students really have a sense that this is a family here... teachers, peers, staff, custodians.

> The first teacher really comes from home with the parents. With the grandmother, an aunt, an uncle.

We teach values. We're a Catholic school. It produces a certain kind of student.

> It makes a very special young lady and young man when they graduate. The school, the church have always stood for something very special. This is community... I think it's all about love.

The bottom line is love. You love the kids. They need support. They need constant work. They need drill. They need someone who is going to get them focused on their work and say, yes, you can do it.

> I enjoy [seeing] success. When they can focus, when they see that result... that ultimate goal, that future.

On a daily basis, I love it when my students accomplish their tasks and feel good about it. 'Cause that's just going to lead to more success. It's going to make them walk into Yvonne's class [and] succeed and feel good about themselves. That's basically what I'm after.

DOUGLAS BRETT

St. Augustine School of the Arts is a parochial school, grades kindergarten through eight. It is not an arts magnet, but rather offers an arts-based education.

Piano/Vocal
St. Augustine School of the Arts
The Bronx, New York

YVONNE RHEM-TITTLE

Science/Math/Career Studies
St. Augustine School of the Arts
The Bronx, New York

Start Over

If you want to change American education for the better, you can't put Band-Aids all over the problems. You basically have to take a bulldozer and run all over it and start all over again.

George Guthridge
Alaska

I think the public is misinterpreting restructuring. It's not playing around the edges and saying, "Well, we'll have lunch after recess." That's not restructuring at all. A lot of teachers have no idea what it is. A lot of administrators have no idea what it is. I would like to see as much control left with local school boards, local school districts, local buildings as possible. That's where you impact the kids. Because then you're talking to the people, the teachers and the parents who know them best. It's the belief system. It's the values that you hold dear, that your whole group holds dear. You build on that. You don't say, "Well, we have a seven-period day. Make everything fit." No. You say, "What's really important to us? What do we want kids to be able to do? What do we want them to know? How can we best do that?" Then you build the structure on top of your beliefs. We are still working backwards.

Pamela Adams Johnson
Iowa

Let's take five days for a retreat for each school staff. That includes teachers and administrators and counselors and the school lunchroom people and the custodians and the secretaries and the teachers' aides. Every adult in the building who deals with those students. Let's go away from the school [for] five days and ask ourselves a couple of questions. First of all, what are the specific needs of our population of students? Whatever age they are, whatever abilities they have, whatever neighborhood they come from. What do our students need, not just academically, but all the . . . needs they have. What do they need to be successful students and successful in life? Once we get that question answered, let's look at the education research — recent, the last 10 to 15 years. What methods have been proven to meet those needs of that kind of student? Third question, what particular gifts and talents and abilities do we as a staff and as individuals possess? OK, very simple. Now how can we take our particular gifts, our building space and our time — and let's look beyond the time of the regular school day to all the time we can use — how can we use ourselves, our space, our time to meet all of those needs? That would work. Every school would come up with a unique plan that's designed just for its own specific students. No two schools in the country would be alike, but they'd all be meeting the students' needs and so all of their students would be successful. Teachers would feel great, that they are really able to use their skills in a positive way. Students would feel great because they are succeeding. That would be fantastic. . . . Do it. Get the parents on your side. It may take some political organizing. It may take some public relations. Do whatever it takes.

Billy Dean Nave, Jr.
Maine

Let Teachers Teach

Let's treat all teachers as individuals. It bothers me sometimes when we say we have to all teach the same because I'm not the same as the guy in the next room. Let's recognize individual differences. And allow teachers to fail once in a while. I'm not talking about a terminal failure. But I'm saying the only way we can be successful is to fail once in a while because success is overcoming failure. It was Edison that said if we're not failing once in a while, we're not being very innovative. I know that when I have a bad lesson or things don't go well, hey, we can can that one. That wasn't a good idea. But the only way we can find out what really works is to do some experimentation in our classroom with a new concept that we are going to be introducing to the students. And the greatest evaluators are the students themselves.

Bill Collar
Wisconsin

There's no one method or one style, as you know. Every teacher teaches different styles. I have great faith. I am an optimist. I'm kind of prejudiced. The greatest group in the world is the group of teachers because they give so much of themselves. So I [hope] that the people in hierarchy will kind of back off and stop giving all these ultimatums and rules and guidelines and get back to the real teacher in the classroom. Can we find a way? So you can help me, so I can help you, so we can help the child?

Yvonne Rhem-Tittle
New York

I've learned a lot from peers, too. Like the lady that came from the Bronx when I first started teaching. Anytime I needed help, she was there. She's a real traditional teacher, very strict, very organized. I was the opposite, and I've learned a great deal from her. I like her way of teaching . . . She was a great teacher. But I won't go out and pretend to teach [that way]. I will just use whatever she gives me the best I can. We teachers should have that freedom. To teach the way we think as long as we get good quality education for the students.

Wilma F. Mad Plume
Montana

Teachers have taken a bad rap. You're expected to be too many things right now. Doctor, lawyer, psychiatrist, psychologist. If they would let teachers teach and not worry about all the other things, the school district would be able to get the kids' scores up. Spending time with discipline reports [and] all the other paperwork that comes down from the district. That's the biggest thing. If teachers could just be allowed to teach and not have to worry about all the other outside influences.

Ronald G. Suvak, Sr.
Pennsylvania

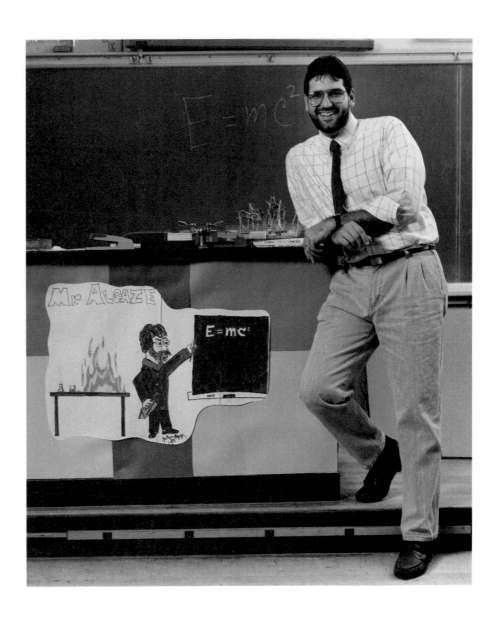

LOUIS ALGAZE

General Science, seventh grade
West Miami Junior High School
Miami, Florida

The schools aren't here for the teachers. They're here for the students. They're not here for the principal, they're not here for the administrator, they're not here for the teachers, but for the students. Sometimes people lose sight of that fact.

VERLEETA WOOTEN

World History II/World History III/U. S. History
West Seattle High School
Seattle, Washington

What's my job all about? My job is all about those kids who walk into my door every day. My job is about introducing them to the world, to the world of learning and all those joys that are out there for them. I want to do it well and make a difference for the kids.

WILMA F. MAD PLUME

Ms. Mad Plume is a Native American of the Blackfeet tribe.

Second grade
Vina Chattin School/Blackfeet Indian Reservation
Browning, Montana

My husband and I married very young. I'm still in love with him the way I was when I met him. We didn't really have role models back then. It was just being able to get by from day to day. Education was put aside . . . But knowing that I had my own children, I had to make a good life for them. We had to pick ourselves up and go find our goals and complete them. . . .

I was a housewife, and my son started kindergarten. I began to want to be something more. I started school, and I went to our Blackfeet Community College. I graduated from there, then went to the University of Montana. I received my Elementary Education degree in 1985 . . . .

I have real high expectations of my students, and they know that. I like to teach a child as a whole, not just teach them how to write and read and do math . . . Someday Johnny might come to school hungry. Maybe Johnny's dad left him. I watch out for things like that. I guess I'm kind of a protective teacher. I know they are vulnerable. I know I play a role in their lives . . . I understand what they're going through.

VIRGIL WILKINS

Agricultural Education
Hundred High School
Hundred, West Virginia

I think the teacher has to have certain traits
that are enticing. You have to think and act
like a teacher. You should be a knowledgeable
person. You have to be well-trained. You have
to prove yourself as a teacher. When you have
those characteristics going for you, students
believe what you are doing is valuable.

Our school enrollment is about 180 students.
My enrollment per year averages about 93
or 94. So we get 50 percent of our student body
into Vocational Agriculture, boys and girls
included. I am very satisfied that we can draw
that many.

PETER OLESEN LUND

Industrial Arts Technology Education
Timberlane Regional Middle School
Plaistow, New Hampshire

Traditional industrial arts filled a need in terms
of the Industrial Revolution, teaching people
how to run machinery. We now need people to
do more than just run machinery. We need
them to be able to troubleshoot, to set up
a series of operations or design robotic
movements to correlate to an industrial
process. That was never part of my growing up.
It's very much a part of today.

DAVID ANSTAETT

Creative Writing, seventh grade
Center of Differentiated Education
Smith Hale Junior High School
Hickman Mills, Missouri

They're awesome. I never had a student that
wasn't awesome. You have to understand
that . . . because students are motivating.
They're stimulating . . . They're challenging.
They won't tolerate us not knowing.

ROBERTA FORD

Language Arts
Prairie Middle School
Cherry Creek School District
Aurora, Colorado

Why do I teach? Because I was born to do it.
That's the only way I can answer you. I think
I came out with chalk in my hand.

GEORGE GUTHRIDGE

Mr. Guthridge teaches in a village 90 miles east of Nome, Alaska. He has coached teams of Eskimo students to national championships in academic competitions three times.

Reading/English/Social Studies
Aniguiim High School
Elim, Alaska

My kids won the Future Problem Solving National Championships . . . We got on a plane in a blizzard on the edge of the Arctic and went into Anchorage. A couple of my kids had never been to a hotel. Most had never been in an elevator. They beat the smartest kids in Alaska. Then they beat the smartest kids in the States. It's pretty phenomenal . . . So I sat down and reviewed how we had done it.

The trend the last 20 years in American education has been to spark students' interest with creativity, then show the larger picture. Conceptualization, then familiarization, then memorization. I reversed that. Memorization first, then familiarization, then the bigger picture. Creativity comes last. So they're able to operate from that knowledge base . . . instead of just, well, here's a concept and here's a concept . . .

It's a lot like the way kids learn how to hunt. Not just in the old days. Kids in rural situations do just about everything the same way. The first thing they do is memorize. They shut up and watch . . . The second thing they do is familiarize themselves with the tool. There's a good reason why Eskimo boys are good hunters. I mean they know that rifle. Then they conceptualize [and] think about the larger picture like why the whales come in when they do . . . The relationship between the ice pattern and the seal migration. Then after all that's done, after they become a successful hunter, then they become creative. Everything is perfectly thought out because if you're creative out on the ice, you'll die. A simple mistake will kill you . . .

From that I've slowly built up the way I teach. It's not the only way, but we just drill and drill and drill. Almost everything is done by lecture . . . What is ironic is [that] I think, God, my classes are boring. And yet all of the kids, almost without exception, will tell you that my class is the most interesting . . . They know they're getting a lot of information.

I have made a point a lot of times when I teach teachers that innovation without foundation is like a deck of cards built on a sand dune. I have seen so many teachers that give all these innovative ideas, but the kids . . . don't even know where Europe is. When you come out of my class, you know that subject.

K A R E N   H U D S O N   A S H B R O O K

Homebound
Ohio County Schools
Wheeling, West Virginia

I teach homebound students. Kids who are unable to be in school for medical reasons, emotional reasons, occasionally court orders. If they are not able to be in school, then they are on a homebound basis . . . I work one-on-one . . . [with] about 75 students a year. Every student I have has a problem, or the student would not be out of the regular classroom. But they are still entitled to an education. . . .

I get a lot of students who have illnesses and aren't expected to make it past a certain age. They invariably fool everybody and go farther. I'd like to think that part of that is because we care enough to keep schooling them. In their minds, there's always some hope. The children think, why would they bother with school for me if I wasn't going to make it? Sometimes it helps them make it a little longer . . . I've got maybe four leukemia students who are now declared cured.

Parents

The first teacher really comes from home with the parents. With the grandmother. With an aunt, with an uncle. Or teaching how to thread a needle or sitting down and listening to a father play a harmonica. There's so much. There are more than just teachers that get a degree, you see.

Yvonne Rhem-Tittle
New York

We need more parent involvement. When I spoke to the principal of the junior high school, I said, "If we are going to make a difference here, and if we are going to talk about restructuring and getting closer to the student, we need to get the parents involved." We all have to be involved in a support system for kids. I guess that's it, a strong support system. I think that's what we need. The way our schools are structured now, kids move at the high school level — junior high, too — in 47-minute blocks. Forty-seven minutes, boom, they are going to another teacher. There could be something very wrong in that kid's life that's keeping him from achieving, and we would not know that . . . We have no contact with the parents unless we call the parent. Months could go by before anybody would know that kid was in trouble.

Grace Hall McEntee
Rhode Island

It helps [to know the parents]. Because parents know what I expect, and I find that so many of them tell me, "I'll be glad when Johnny gets in your class. I told him what you expect. He knows he's going to have to work."

I find also that when Johnny doesn't live up to his mom's expectations or mine, parents immediately jump in. "Well, yes, Johnny's going to have to do better."

Bettye McLaughlin
Arkansas

I teach [parents] how to ask the right questions. Many of them are already saying, "Do you have any homework?" Or, "How was school today?" The conversation ends right there. The kid will usually give them a one-word answer, and it's over. The parents heard what they want to hear, and the student's off the hook until the report card comes. And then everybody says, "Well, what was going on here? I've been asking you every day [about] homework, and now you have F's." [I'm] trying to help parents realize that they need to be persistent in the kinds of questions that they ask.

Instead of, "How was school today?" . . . say, "Well, what did you do in math class today?" And the student may say, "Aw, nothing." Or, "Not much." And then I ask the parent to say, "Well, can you give me an example of the kind of the problem you were working on?" Try to get the student to think specifically about what they were really trying to learn in school. I ask the parent to do that in every subject each day. It takes only a few minutes, but be persistent. If the student says, "Nothing," or, "Not much," be persistent and say, "Well, I just want to know a little bit about what you're doing. Tell me one thing." And to wait and be patient. What I'm after is some kind of carryover . . .

A student who knows what's going on in their class should be able to tell what probably will happen the next day in class. So I ask parents to say, "Well, what do you think you'll do tomorrow? Do you think you'll be having a test?" Because a student should be able to predict. They know then that their parents value their education. Even though parents may value it anyway, the kid doesn't really see that until this questioning starts taking place and more time is spent dealing with what school's all about.

Richard Spry
Tennessee

Many of the children that I teach in this very affluent school district, I wonder how they even get to school in the morning, much less learn anything. We are talking about economic troubles. We're talking about split families . . . . A lot of single parents [are] fighting for economic survival. Last year I was furious because one of my kids was here very, very early in the morning and very, very late at night. And I said, "What does this mother think she's doing? Why isn't she home taking care of that kid?" She came in for a conference and was irate. The steam was pouring out of her nostrils. At the end of the conference, she and I were crying and hugging each other because she had taken the children away from their father when they were three because he was physically abusing them. She was working two jobs, shift work. Doesn't know from one week to the next what her hours are going to be. Sometimes she has to be at work at 4:00 in the morning. That's what we're dealing with. I firmly believe, although I didn't used to think this was true, that it's not a question of choice. It's just the way it has to be. A lot of these parents are fighting for survival.

Roberta Ford
Colorado

I suppose [our kids] are similar to kids anyplace except that we are so close here. I'm from here, and I live just down the road a quarter of a mile. My husband is from here, too, and whoever he's not related to, I'm probably related to. There's so much family that we're probably closer to the kids than teachers other places would be. Because our Indian relationships are different from what you might be familiar with. I have one girl in class now, and she said, "You're my grandma, aren't you?" Well, she's not a child of one of my children. But in our Indian relationships, yes, I am her grandmother. I'm also her aunt in another way. Her mother and I are cousins. And that would make me her aunt in our relations. So I think we're basically closer to our kids. . . .

In discipline I know that I can tell them, "If you get into trouble you'd better tell [your parents] before I do. You'd better tell them right, too." Usually they go home and fess up. Their parents tell them [that they] weren't sent to school to act like that. So, maybe it's not too different from what another teacher might do, anyway. But since we know each other so well and are so close, there's hardly a chance of getting by with anything in school because the parents will hear about it.

Cleo Charging
North Dakota

This would be years ago in my student teaching. The parents had separated very abruptly without the child realizing that there was any problem. Basically an abandonment situation. [This student] was at the seventh grade level, the oldest child in the family, [and] was expected to assume a lot of responsibilities as the remaining parent was trying to deal with his own problems and yet still father three children. The child just enjoyed [my class] and kept coming back for longer and longer periods of time. He obviously would prefer to spend time here in this classroom than go home. And I allowed that to occur. He was a student that just needed some time and someone to talk to him one-on-one. He worked around the lab with me and things of that sort. I did a couple of different activities with him. Maybe two or three times in a month. [One] afternoon we might go shopping with another student or two. On a weekend we might go into Boston for the day or something like that, providing him some one-on-one activities where he was the prime focus and special. I had the opportunity to do that, the time to do that, and he certainly had the need. The parent was supportive and appreciated what I was doing in his trying to bring himself back up to being able to handle the situation. That's created a lifelong friendship with that family.

Peter Olesen Lund
New Hampshire

BILLY DEAN NAVE, Jr.

The River Valley Alternative School is designed to meet the needs of students who have dropped out or have not functioned well within a traditional school setting. Seventy percent of Mr. Nave's students go on to higher education.

Ninth grade through postgraduate
River Valley Alternative School
Turner, Maine

Every single human being is of infinite worth and value and is to be respected and accepted as such, especially kids who have been rejected all their lives. Kids who have been rejected by teachers, rejected by their peers, rejected by families, told that they were less than good people. Those kids in particular respond amazingly to acceptance and respect and love and live up to whatever expectations an accepting person has of them.

JENLANE GEE

Third grade
Christin Siphard Elementary School
Modesto, California

Children feel so disenfranchised. They
don't feel like they belong . . . [that]
they're a part of something. That's
where we have a lot of problems in our
community. Children who don't know
where they belong . . . in a community, in
a neighborhood, in a family. Maybe they
don't know how they fit in. But in this
classroom, I make no doubts about how
they fit in with me.

ELAINE C. CAPOBIANCO

Ms. Capobianco developed and implemented a program called Q.U.I.L.T.S. (Quilts Unite Integrative Logical Thinking Successfully). She used the project to integrate thinking, planning, geometry, history and self-discipline in a kind of "academic artistry." Although her students began with no sewing skills, they later won awards at quilt-making competitions. She is pictured with two students from her first quilting class.

Due to budget cutbacks, Ms. Capobianco has been unable to continue the program and has transferred to a different school.

Elementary
Kenny School
Dorchester, Massachusetts

I started the program in the 1984-85 school year. I walked into this totally dysfunctional middle school. I mean they were break-dancing on tables. It was just incredible. The teacher that was there before me quit. The machines were all broken . . . smashed against walls. And I thought, my God, do I want this job? But I did. Took it one step at a time.

When these kids started to quilt it was really tricky getting them going and keeping them encouraged. That's when I started bringing in more literature about quilts being sold and how valuable they were in history. "This is going to tell somebody a story about you," I said. Then they started to get some spirit.

I'll never forget the day of the [New England Quilters Guild] competition. We went to pick Rodney up at 7:30 in the morning because we had to drive up for the contest. Well, Rodney was [there] at 5:30 in the morning. He was shivering to death when I got there . . . I

thought, this kid stood out for two hours in the cold because he didn't want to be late. That just struck me. What has this done for him that I don't even realize? After he got his award, he turned to me and said, "This is the Grammy Award of quilting." It changed me from then on. I knew that this program had much more impact and more to give.

Kids at school were looking up to Rodney. Wow! Rodney won! He believed in what he could do. I think he felt it. His whole walk was completely different because he had done something for himself. Their class let me know that I was really going to help these kids . . . Giving them the power to do what they wanted to do. I have the knowledge. Tell me what you want to know, and I will show you how to do it.

One time Rodney called me the Miracle Worker. Ms. Capobianco, she's the Miracle Worker. He gave me what I needed as a teacher to take all the crap that you get and the lack of respect. He gave me the courage to keep trying and to say, I'm going to help someone today.

MELISSA ALLOWAY

Deaf Education Teacher
Dallas Regional School for the Deaf
Dallas, Texas

I teach because it challenges me to use my creativity so that I can connect with children and
become part of their lives. They can become
part of my life, and we can grow together.

MIKE HOVEY

Economics/Vocational Marketing
American Falls High School
American Falls, Idaho

I had three seniors who were going to drop out of school, get a job for $3.85 an hour, rent an apartment, live the good life. So I was doing some reading, and by no means is [this] my project. It's just the way that I implemented it. It's a [simulated] payroll grading system. In my classroom there's a time clock and a bunch of time cards. Every kid, when they walk in, they punch in. If they are in class the full period, five days a week, they get a 40-hour check [on] Friday . . . I pay them minimum wage . . . $134.00 a week.

But then we get into "real life." We subtract social security, Idaho income tax, federal income tax. They end up taking home $104.26 after taxes. They pay me $50.00 a week for the desk, $35.00 a week for using the books. That leaves them $19.00 and some cents. And then they make their car payments, their gas, [food], take their dates out, pay for their insurance.

I've had some students say, "Hey, I've got to do something. I can't live on minimum wage. I've got to get myself some skills." You can talk about supply and demand. You can talk about fiscal policy, but if you don't make it real . . .

Tardies? I don't worry about tardies. They're tardy, they get docked an hour's pay.

RICHARD SPRY

Fourth grade
J. E. Moss Elementary School
Nashville, Tennessee

Learning about caring for our world is an easy way for kids to focus on coming out of themselves. It's hard to be a selfish person and work with the environment and do recycling and those kinds of projects. So, they are getting away from themselves. It helps them to deal with each other in a different way. And if you're going to care about your environment and the world, usually there is a lot of carryover in the way you deal with other people. You see them as more valuable also.

ERNESTINE HOGAN

Math
Southside Comprehensive High School
Atlanta, Georgia

Sometimes teachers get lazy, and they want to teach everybody the same way. You lose a lot of students like that because you are not . . . I hate to say this, but you're not teaching. You really aren't teaching. A lot of people want to teach, but there's a difference between teaching and inspiring, a difference in instructing and enlightening. There's a difference.

MARILYN GILLIS

Health/Home Economics
Milton Junior-Senior High School
Milton, Vermont

Home economics education today is focusing on human development, consumer skills, management skills. And I teach human relationships and human sexuality. I think it's one of the most important things that kids need today. Teenagers are living in a tough world. They need information about their own development. So I really believe that what I teach is important because kids tell me. If you are a parent, you can't prevent your child from getting sex education — not if you let them out of your house. Not if you have a television. Not if you have a radio. Not if you let them listen to music. . . .

One of the school board members wanted only "pure" home economics taught here, which is of course cooking and sewing. Some of these parents [have said], "Well, we shouldn't be teaching this stuff. They are too young to hear this stuff." If those people could see some of the questions that I get asked anonymously by seventh graders, it would probably make their hair curl.

JOHANNA BROWN

Math
Swartz Creek Middle School
Swartz Creek, Michigan

We have a whole society that's been math brutalized. Whole generations who do not understand math... We exposed them to material they didn't have a knowledge base for or presented it to them in a boring way. Or it could be a personal degradation. People who have experienced math brutality can tell you who, when, where and what they were wearing when they were belittled or threatened or punished... We said women aren't supposed to be able to do math, so they thought, why bother? We told students that fractions are awful, so they put them aside and thought, I'll never get those.

I see it more in the adults that I teach at the university level because they admit it's happened to them. A man said, "I went to take statistics at the university a year ago, and all the math phobia came back. I'm 55 years old, successful in [business]. And I froze. I was a little kid again, right back in that box."

Kids still try to cover it up. The sensitive student withdraws. The overt student misbehaves because they would rather be obnoxious than be thought stupid and incapable.

Math teachers that teach by divine revelation never understand what their end product is like. "You don't understand? If you weren't given it genetically, you'll never get it."

That really offends me. We're not going to get to the top of the heap, America. I want the best for my children. I want the best for these children.

We've lost sight, I'm sorry. I don't want to criticize my fellow teacher. I don't want to criticize myself, but....

We think we can't make mistakes. Teachers tend to do that... I think we have a right to learn from mistakes... I allow people to see me make mistakes, to convey that I am human... "Okay, what did I do? What can we learn from my mistake?"

When I finished giving finals at the University of Michigan at Flint, people came up and touched me on the shoulder and said, "You've freed me from the bonds that have held me back from learning math."

That's the mystique of the double-edged sword of math. If you don't know it, it's almost like a curse. But you can also raise someone's self-esteem through math because of the tremendous regard people have for it.

Roger's Big Moment

After the seminar in class, I was in the library doing some work. One of the fellows who really struggles — he is learning disabled and he doesn't have much confidence in himself — stopped by my chair. He said, "Did you grade the seminar yet?"

"No," I said, "you haven't graded yourself yet." The students grade themselves, and I grade them, then we average the two together. "What do you deserve in seminar today, Roger?"

He said, "Well, I really did my best. I think I did pretty well."

And I said, "Well, what do you deserve?"

"I don't know. What do you think?"

"Wait a minute," I said. "Suppose we were grading one to five — one being the best, five being the worst. What do you think you deserve?" Again, he couldn't answer. "Five? Do you think you deserve five, which is the worst?"

He said, "No, no. I think I did very well."

"Do you think you deserve a one?"

He smiled, [but] he didn't say yes. He said, "I have to tell you something. This is the first time that I have ever understood what somebody else thought when they thought something different than me."

I said, "Wow," and I shook his hand. "Wow, Roger, that's great."

He said, "I didn't really change my mind about what I thought, but when Robert was talking, I understood what Robert meant. And I understood how he felt. That's the first time."

"Well, what do you deserve for the seminar, Roger? Do you deserve a one?"

"Yeah, I think I deserve a one."

"Do you think you participated in that conversation, and it was worth a one?"

"Yeah."

"OK. I think it was a one, also."

That was Roger's big moment. That's his biggest moment in education, in twelve years, or however many years he had been going to school. And it was wonderful for me as a teacher. I went home, and I was ready to leap around, I was so happy. Because for us as teachers, that's a wonderful thing. To have a student say this is the first time ever that I understood. Wow. Anyway, Roger's writing is better from that moment, too. Why I don't know. But he has decided now, here it is April, [that] he's going to graduate next month.

Grace Hall McEntee
Rhode Island

Could You Please Stop Talking?

This is a good story. In fact, this is what made this program permanent in my mind.

The most successful program that I run in my English class is a silent reading program. The students choose their own books. My first year of teaching, I had five sections of basic English—kids who cannot read, cannot write, cannot pass another class. That's all I taught all day long. Reading, writing, grammar. Basic skills, sort of survival skills.

I started working with these kids and I asked them, "How many of you have a bookshelf at home that's filled with books?" No hands. "How many of you have seen your parents read a book?" No hands. "How many of you see your parents read a newspaper or magazine on a regular basis?" A few hands. And I realized here are a hundred plus students coming into my room each day who never see an adult read. They see adults do all kinds of other things, and they need to see an adult read. So, we sat down and read, and they saw me read. We talked about what we were reading. It was very informal, trying to draw some interest for reading.

I was doing this reading program, and the principal came into the room. For ten or twelve minutes or whatever it was, there was no interaction. There was silence. He left the room and called me into his office later and said, "What was going on there?" I explained this program and why I did it. He said, "Can you really justify not teaching those ten or twelve minutes at the beginning of the hour?" I tried to explain to him [that] they need an adult reader model. And I am being that model.

As a first-year teacher, of course, asking me to justify what I was doing, I spent some serious days after that. Am I really doing the right thing? Maybe I am making a mistake. Maybe I'm just a beginner, and I don't really know what I'm doing.

One day, not long after this, I was talking to the kids and I was explaining some upcoming assignments, just scheduling kinds of things. A kid raised his hand and asked, "Could you please stop talking? You are cutting into our reading time."

And I thought, "That's it!" I had all the proof I needed. It made a difference to this kid. He wanted to read.

I never did convince the principal. He was the only principal I ever had who didn't think it was a very good use of class time.

Steve Gardiner
Wyoming

LYNN A. WILHELM

General Science, seventh and eighth grades
Custer Baker Middle School
Franklin, Indiana

We talk about why animals become extinct and
why species become endangered. Any kid in
any of my classes can tell you it's because of loss
of habitat. That's why we lose certain species.
Loss of habitat... So by teaching about ecology
and conservation and the environment, you are
showing the kids that we have to take care of
our natural resources. Because if we don't, we
will lose our habitat. And they know exactly
what happens if an animal loses its habitat.
It means the species does not survive.

You can make it so that they really understand.

BILL COLLAR

Mr. Collar has coached a state championship football team and has often been invited to present seminars on the teaching of social studies.

U.S. History/Great Issues/Head Football and Track Coach
Seymour High School
Seymour, Wisconsin

My ego has gotten smaller and smaller over the years. It used to be when I was a young coach, if we lost, my wife would rush home and hide all the sharp objects. I still take it very seriously . . . I'm very competitive. I love to win . . . But I realize it's still just a game played by high school youth. I think sometimes it gets a little out of perspective.

It's so easy to slip into that mode of the emotionalism involved in the game rather than the lasting benefit of the experiences that a person might have in the classroom as well as the positive characteristics that can be associated with the team.

JORGE "COCO" VAZQUEZ

Special Education
Box Elder Junior High School
Brigham City, Utah

This program started as the need for an adaptive physical-education program . . . Regular physical-education activities were either too demanding or not at all suited for their needs. Just by accident, my training in karate and my training in special-education brought this program about. Not only did it become an adaptive physical-education program, but a total intervention program . . . Through the karate classroom model, we're able to deliver all the services that [special-education] children need within a school setting. Working on their social skills, their behavioral adjustments, study skills. Learning how to pay attention. Learning to listen . . . We teach the kids how to relax, how to focus, how to maintain attention.

The kids come, change into their uniforms, do some stretching exercises. We do a concentration exercise in which we review mentally all of the prior things that we've done [for example] in math . . . just working with our own imaginations and self-talk. We say, "These are the things we are going to do today. See the problem. Imagine yourself doing it. Imagine yourself doing it well. Being happy. Being strong. Being good." We do a few karate techniques, then we break up into desk work. Within short periods of time they become quite able.

With this approach, the attitude changes. Once the attitude changes, the behavior takes care of itself. It's not the karate . . . itself. The karate is a motivational [vehicle]. . . .

Most of these kids have been battered by either the system or by the stereotype. In most other schools you fight the fact that most of the school is down on the special-ed kids . . . They are ostracized . . . I tell the students I don't care what's happened in your past. When you come to me, you're not coming as a label. You're coming as an individual. The only thing you're going to learn from now on is how to succeed . . . I'm not going to give you anything. You're going to earn it. It's a reality-based approach, a no-nonsense approach. The rewards are immediate because they start seeing the changes in themselves. . . .

We have kids that are not special-ed kids that want to come to the program . . . My kids interact at the same clout level as the rich kids, the best wrestlers, the best football players. When they walk out in the halls they are respected here. The kids just eat that up.

ELAINE MATSUZAKI

Ms. Matsuzaki is a veteran of 29 years in the classroom. She has recently been involved in bringing change to the curriculum and structure of her school. These include interdisciplinary teams, heterogeneous grouping and cooperative learning.

Math
Castle High School
Honolulu, Hawaii

If you are not happy [with] the way things are going, then you need to do something about it. It's got to be positive. It has to be changing yourself first. I like to try new things. It's a big risk . . . [but] I never think about the risk and failure because I'm a problem solver . . . You have to constantly refocus. Look at what you're doing. Reflect. Are you satisfied?

Just the other day I was driving home and I thought, you know, it doesn't feel the same. I don't feel burned out. I don't feel overworked. It feels different . . . like it's not as exhausting although we work harder. I really enjoy teaching this year.

BETTYE McLAUGHLIN

Senior English/AP English
Bald Knob High School
Bald Knob, Arkansas

Dreams. I hope that they will take their dreams and know that they can fulfill those dreams if they will fulfill the potential that is in them. And I hope that I have helped them to know what that potential is . . . that they can do great and marvelous things if they'll use their minds.

Burnout

I think sabbaticals need to be easier for people to get. In our district you can get a sabbatical after you've taught seven years, but you go at half salary. Well, you cannot take a sabbatical, go to school and live on half salary. Because part of that year you spend stressing out: How I am going to make it through the year? There are a lot of us who have passed the seven years for sabbatical and have never taken them because of the compensation . . . .

When a teacher is beginning to stress out, give them the assistance that they need to refresh themselves. If what they need to do is transfer to another school or a different level, give them the training that they need. Don't just say, "Well, you're through. We're going to hire somebody new to take your place." They are valuable people. They've been there a long time. They know the system. They know how to work with kids. They just need a new lease on their professional life.

Verleeta Wooten
Washington

[It] troubles me because I see a lot of people that have burned out. I see it on the left of me and on the right of me. My only advice to them is [that] I wish they would get out. Because I think it's bad for kids. Kids need to see fighters. They need to see people that are enthusiastic. Some people say society demands too much of teachers. I can't argue with that, but at the same time I think as teachers we can't forget what our job is supposed to be.

Edward J. Wong
Mississippi

I think burnout happens when you get hung up and overly concerned about the things that shouldn't matter, don't matter. You get focused on them. And after it's all over, you realize, hey, focus on the kids. That's what counts. When I have stress, when I get upset, I am the most relaxed coming into my class. I want to get back to my class. Long as I'm with the kids, I feel very relaxed, safe. They understand. They see me every day, my whole day, with the honesty and passion that I have . . . Sometimes you get so hung up on the outside stuff . . . but the kids understand.

Michelle Peck
Wyoming

Burnout? I'm too busy to think about it.

Ronald G. Suvak, Sr.
Pennsylvania

Want to Trade Places?

I'm a teacher. You almost want to mumble it because people say, "What, you're a teacher?" But it's also funny because people will say to me, "Ah! You've got such a soft job, three months off. What a great job you have!" I'll turn around and ask, "Would you like to trade places with me?"

Inevitably they say, "No way." They think that I've got it so neat, but would they trade places with me? There's no way they would do that.

Linda K. Hillestad
South Dakota

There are times that the outside doesn't respect teachers. You're at a party sometimes, and everyone is a stockbroker or a computer whiz or whatever, and you say, "I'm a teacher." And they go, "Oh, a teacher. You don't work in the summer." I think that there's a point in time where even though you know you're doing something meaningful, society might not deem it as valuable as they should. It gets discouraging sometimes.

W. Dean Eastman
Massachusetts

I believe that teachers do not quite command the respect that they did 30 years ago. People question teachers sometimes, and parents do not back them up quite as much as they used to. This is true, and it's too bad. But it is true.

Ruth Jean Andersen
Kansas

I think a lot of it goes back to how teachers perceive themselves first . . . I feel like I'm really making a difference. I think the reason I feel that way is because there's so much validation and bombardment going on right now, from our President to our community, to the corporations out there who are throwing money at us to try to help us . . . So all of a sudden we've got that support again where it's not just the negative that you keep hearing about — the drug problems and the dropouts and the teenage suicide and all the other issues going on in the community that are coming into our classrooms. I think it's coming around. There's just more of an awareness now . . . It goes back to that sense of self-esteem. You have to work on what the positive is because nobody wants to be told what they're doing wrong. We all admit that we've failed in some way, but we have to learn from our failures and move on. We want to know what's working, too.

Jenlane Gee
California

There's a definite difference between the teaching profession here and the teaching profession abroad. I was in Hungary in 1988, International Congress on Education. It's hard to communicate the most important things I learned. But . . . two things. First of all the status of the teacher is much higher. I mean the Italian word . . . Italian kids call their teacher "Maestro." That says it all. Right? We don't have [that]. What do we say, "Hey, teach? . . . Mr. So and So." But there is something else about being a teacher in this country which is different from other places. American society, I think, values aggressiveness. Go out and get 'em. And teaching, the way it's structured now, there's not a whole lot of that built into the profession. They need teachers to be docile. Not to be aggressive. To be good but not too good. Otherwise they have to pay them more.

Mark Saul
New York

MARY LAYCOCK

Ms. Laycock has been teaching math for 52 years. The first 30 years were spent in the public schools of Oak Ridge, Tennessee, site of the Oak Ridge National Laboratory. For the past 22 years she has been at the Nueva Learning Center, a private school for gifted children, including those with learning disabilities. Ms. Laycock moved to California when her assistant superintendent at Oak Ridge became the first director of the Nueva Learning Center. He asked her to "create a program that teaches mathematics instead of arithmetic from day one." Ms. Laycock has throughout her career developed innovative ways to teach math. She has conducted workshops on the teaching of math in 49 of the 50 states.

Math
Nueva Center for Learning
Hillsborough, California

I have been at this 52 years. [When] I was in Oak Ridge, you can imagine the population I dealt with...tremendous scientists and gifted kids.

We [also] had kids that could not read the basic math book. There was no middle. They were either A's and B's or D's.

I said, "You give those low kids to me." So every year I had that class, kids who couldn't read the book. I sewed for my [children]— that was the only way I could make ends meet —and I had lots of spools. So I dyed them. Ten spools green, ten spools white...'til I had a hundred. That was the way I taught those kids to multiply and divide. Then I got popsicle sticks and put rubber bands around them. A bundle of ten was one-tenth, and ten bundles of ten were a hundred. It worked, and those kids got to the point where they could do the ordinary thing about what a tip is or how much their tax was. They had built that multiplication table with [sticks] and spools. So they had experienced it....

[When] they think about the meaning of the operation, that is mathematics. Arithmetic is just to be able to spout the right answer. That is why our testing has to be changed. We are just evaluating teachers and kids in getting right answers on the arithmetic. We must evaluate them in such a way that [they] can give evidence that they understand what they are doing. And we have to train teachers to do that.

Teaching isn't telling people things. It's asking questions. I want them to have kids discover rather than tell them anything. I never want a child told a rule. They must touch something so that out of touching and doing the kid makes the rule rather than being told to memorize the rules...I will not tell them if they are right or wrong. They have to prove it. And then they know because they have touched it and worked it out for themselves. And that is really, really important...Some children say, "Just tell me how to do this and let me do it." I say, "OK, but before you get through with it, you have to prove it to me." And they will memorize like crazy 'cause they are used to that. But then I won't let them rest until they can prove to me why it is true.

I don't get tired as long as I do math...Look how stimulating the kids are. And that is true of any kid if you know how to read what is going on in their heads. I love every minute I'm with the kids. I'm on the edge of making sense out of math and making it fun. Get excited. I have got a new game I can't wait to share.

GAIL McCREADY STAGGERS

Ms. Staggers has been teaching at the High School in the Community for 17 years. It was established as a teacher-run school in 1972. Teachers handle the administrative tasks.

History/Social Studies
High School in the Community
New Haven, Connecticut

I think a lot of cities are headed toward more teacher-involved schools. When people start to feel that they have more at stake than just being there, they feel more responsible. You get a lot more out of people that way . . . .

I think you learn as you go. We do a lot of team-teaching, and I was in no way prepared to do team-teaching when we first decided to do that . . . It's like being married. You have to find time for each other [and] find time to plan. Learn how to cooperate. Work through some things. It also makes you understand that there are other people working toward the same goal and that you are not all by yourself.

JO FRANCIS

Human Relations/European History
Glen Burnie Senior High School
Glen Burnie, Maryland

It's hard to keep your spirits up, really. A
sense of humor is essential. A sense of humor
is a sense of the bigger picture . . . When
something absolutely horrendous is happening
in your classroom on that particular day, the
sense that it's one day and one moment and
that the whole picture is . . . so much greater
than that.

Any Final Thoughts?

Love your kids.

Jaime Escalante
California

I don't accept anything but their best.

Bettye McLaughlin
Arkansas

Let teachers teach.

Ronald G. Suvak, Sr.
Pennsylvania

We can't do it by ourselves.

Teresa R. de Garcia
Colorado

The children are always going to be worth whatever it takes.

Philip Dail
North Carolina

Our future is so important, and children need people that are unique and special and enthusiastic and have the gift to be able to teach. So if it's a question of dedication or life-style, hang in there and stay dedicated.

I see it happen with many good teachers because it's just hard. It's hard work. Sometimes I think education really takes a beating because we don't see the people that are doing wonderful things.

There are lots of wonderful teachers. Hang in there. We need you.

Lynn M. Macal
Minnesota

You have to keep the faith. You really have to. Because somewhere along the line something is really germinating there. And when you plant seeds for 20 years, you have a very big crop. You have a very, very big crop.

Robert H. Sinclair
New York

MARILYN ADEN, page 42;
involved in environmental education with city program called Earthscope; also involved with Burritt Museum Natural History Camp; earned B.S. degree from University of North Dakota New School of Behavioral Studies.

REED ADLER, page 16;
because of his rural situation, Mr. Adler was contacted regarding this book via a neighbor's radio; students come from as far as ten miles away; some have to cross Eagle Creek four times while making their way to school; 20 year teaching veteran; graduate of Long Beach State College.

LOUIS ALGAZE, page 81;
participant in innovative program called TRIP (Teacher Recruitment Incentive Program), established cooperatively by Dade County Public Schools, University of Miami and local teacher organization; college graduates are recruited and become salaried teachers while attending UM on scholarship; successful completion brings a teacher's certificate and master's degree.

PEGGY ALLAN, page 18;
currently on sabbatical as a result of being awarded Illinois State Teacher of the Year; working on doctorate at Southern Illinois University; work is focused on the middle school and restructuring; has devoted her career to middle school level; brother and sister are also teachers.

MELISSA ALLOWAY, page 98;
has taught deaf children in Mexico as well as the U.S.; also conducts workshops for teachers; winner of Ross Perot Award for Excellence in Teaching and PTA Terrific Teacher; married, with "one precious daughter."

RUTH JEAN ANDERSEN, page 61;
having taught elementary school in the same small community for 33 years, she has had a profound influence on literacy there; her mother's experiences as a one-room school teacher in rural Kansas inspired Ms. Andersen to teach.

GLORIA ANDERSON, page 13;
her mother is a retired teacher; her husband, brother and sisters are also educators; 22 years in the classroom; 1990 Virginia Teacher of the Year; Franklin County Chamber of Commerce Award for Community Service; Distinguished Alumni Citation from National Association for Equal Opportunity in Higher Education.

DAVID ANSTAETT, page 86;
a published author of everything from poetry to computer programs; his students are also widely published; described as, "Robin Williams in the classroom"; extremely entertaining and high energy; offers workshops throughout the U.S.; honored often for his teaching, including Paul Witty Award for Contributions to Literature.

KAREN HUDSON ASHBROOK, page 91;
has taught in non-traditional situations for the majority of her 20 year career; has been a homebound teacher for 14 years; received 1987 Youth Services System Community Service Award; husband and sister are both teachers; pictured with a student at his home.

CHARLENE BICE, page 26;
a veteran of 29 years; active in her church and community; named Ft. Worth ISD Teacher of the Year in 1988-89; known as enthusiastic and tireless spokesperson for teaching profession.

DOUGLAS BRETT, page 77;
besides carrying a full teaching load, is also a professional musician and performs full-length classical piano recitals; ten year teaching veteran; holds bachelor's and master's of music degrees from the Manhattan School of Music; plans to pursue doctorate in fall of 1990.

JOHANNA BROWN, page 105;
coordinates Project Aware, introducing both teachers and students to high-tech workplace and requirements for success there; since 1983 has worked with UAW-GM Quality Education Program bringing teachers into plants to assist with training; received 1990 Governor's Superstar Award.

MARGARET BROWN, page 17;
teaches mathematics and science, grades nine through twelve; recipient of numerous awards; is presently involved in efforts to consolidate and revamp existing educational alternative programs for pregnant and parenting teenagers in Caddo Parish where her mother and aunts were also pioneer educators.

ELAINE C. CAPOBIANCO, page 97;
teaches computer technology, grades one through five; honored as Lucretia Crocker Fellow, an exemplary program providing outstanding teachers the opportunity to present their projects and share their ideas with other teachers; recognized by School Committee of City of Boston for innovative instructional programs.

CLEO CHARGING, page 70;
first love is math; teaches a special course on self-esteem to sixth graders; numerous recognitions include: Teacher of the Year, North Dakota Indian Education Association; Classroom Computer Learning/IBM; Outstanding Educator Award, University of North Dakota.

BILL COLLAR, page 109;
teaches classes in motivation and goal setting at University of Wisconsin at LaCrosse; 1985 Wisconsin Football Coach of the Year and 1988 Wisconsin Teacher of the Year; 24 years' experience; member of Seymour Historical Society, has produced videos on local history.

J. J. CONNOLLY, page 44;
has taught for part or all of six decades; missed only three days in 41 years because of sickness; May 18, 1989, was proclaimed J.J. Connolly Day in Texas by governor; wrote school Alma Mater and fight song; five school yearbook dedications; veteran of World War II.

LORRAINE "SAMMY" CRAWFORD, page 59;
coming from a family of teachers, "Sammy" Crawford says, "I believe it is the most honorable of all the professions…;" one of four finalists for National Teacher of the Year, 1988; president of local League of Women Voters; sponsors Model U.N. Club and National Honor Society.

PHILIP DAIL, page 74;
currently involved in project funded by National Science Foundation to write resource guide for beginning chemistry teachers; spent five weeks in summer of 1989 in USSR as adviser to students on science exchange program; 19 years' experience; many former students have become science teachers.

TERESA R. DE GARCIA, page 67;
most challenging experience was having nine children in class speaking nine different languages, none of which was Spanish, plus other students who spoke only English; along with husband, who is also a teacher, presents workshops on parent involvement; 1989 Colorado Educator Award.

W. DEAN EASTMAN, page 22;
has received the Christa McAuliffe Fellowship, the JFK Library Award for Outstanding Teaching of the American Presidency and Certificate of Recognition from Massachusetts Department of Education; once coached in Mexico for U.S. State Department as a Goodwill Ambassador to their Olympic athletes.

DEBI EDWARDS, page 42;
has taught first through eighth grades "in the country, the city and the inner city;" sponsors student government and honor society; active at church; teaches aerobics; member of Huntsville City Swim Team; has "wonderful, supportive husband, two children, ages five and three, and 100 super kids at school."

JIM EISENHARDT, page 21;
honored as Nebraska Drama Teacher of the Year, Northwestern University Graduate Fellow and National Endowment for the Humanities Fellow in Shakespeare; for past 14 years, his students have worked with a professional theatre company to present "A Christmas Carol" to over 40,000 Omaha students free of charge.

JAIME ESCALANTE, page 15;
has received over 100 awards; member of President Bush's Educational Policy Advisory Committee; native of Bolivia where he began his teaching career; has remained in the classroom despite huge demand for speeches and appearances; working on a new video series designed to motivate kids toward math and technical careers.

ROBERTA FORD, page 87;
has taught at all grade levels from elementary to college; active spokesperson for teaching profession; has testified before state legislature; sponsors Adopt-A-Grandparent Club and Project Mankind, designed to involve students in meeting community needs; husband is assistant principal; 1990 Colorado Teacher of the Year.

JO FRANCIS, page 119;
taught English as a Foreign Language, American History, and Western music and drama in Thailand from 1973-77; member of American Psychological Association (High School Teacher Affiliate), Association for Supervision and Curriculum Development and Educators for Social Responsibility; B.A., Swarthmore College, Pennsylvania; M.A., Wesleyan University, Connecticut.

STEVE GARDINER, page 56;
a published author of three books and some 300 articles; helped develop innovative Art and Literature in Nature program; black belt in Taekwondo; received National Endowment for Humanities Fellowship to Harvard; veteran of 13 years; wife, Peggy, teaches also; pictured at library of Teton Science School, Grand Teton National Park.

JENLANE GEE, page 95;
developed and coordinated a drug education program that began in her school and eventually encompassed the entire community; involved with mentor teacher program; provided funding for several scholarships; received California Educator Award; parents, from mainland China, ensured all five of their children got an education.

MARILYN GILLIS, page 102;
conducts workshops for parents and teachers; although human development and sexuality curriculum was state mandated; adverse reaction from some segments of the community made its implementation controversial and difficult; mother was a teacher for over 30 years; proud of her daughter Katie, who is "an excellent student and very involved in service activities."

GEORGE GUTHRIDGE, page 88;
pictured in Nome, Alaska, near the finish line for the 1990 Iditarod dog sled race; published author and member of Science Fiction Writers of America; finalist for Nebula and Hugo Awards for science fiction short stories; his novel *Child of Light* is forthcoming.

JANICE HERBRANSON, page 32;
has taught in rural schools in North Dakota and the Rio Grande Valley of Texas; comes from a family of teachers; 21 years' experience; sponsors local and state chapters of Young Citizens League; has received international publicity due to her rural teaching experiences.

BARBARA HINES HESTER, page 40;
serves on Governor's Task Force for the Arts; has raised an average of $100,000 per year in college scholarships for art students for several years; 1990 Kentucky Teacher of the Year; teaches art to students from Kentucky School for the Blind; organizes student tours to Europe.

LINDA K. HILLESTAD, page 14;
a frequent contributor to textbooks and teachers' guides; was among the 31 teachers selected for Disney's "A Salute to the American Teacher"; 18 year veteran; leads workshops on the teaching of geography; along with other organizations, belongs to Gamma Theta Upsilon, an International Geography Honor Society.

ERNESTINE HOGAN, page 101;
honored many times during her 21 years, including Atlanta Incentive Math Teacher Award and one of three Teacher of the Year finalists for Atlanta area; sponsored a blind student in local and state academic competitions where he won a gold medal; husband is an English teacher at the same school.

TAEKO HORWITZ, page 42;
on Saturdays teaches five different grade levels simultaneously at Japanese Supplementary School for Japanese children living temporarily in U.S.; volunteers for various organizations to build U.S./Japanese relations; husband is physics professor at University of Alabama; their two sons speak Japanese—fluently, of course.

MIKE HOVEY, page 99;
conducts workshops for business educators; has also coached tennis and cross country teams and sponsored rodeo and ski clubs; 1989-90 Idaho Teacher of the Year, among many other honors; wife, Bette, is also an educator; pictured at student-owned school store.

JOHN HOWARTH, page 54;
conducts workshops nationally on the teaching of science, with emphasis on use of computers in laboratory; U.S. representative at International Council of Associations of Science Education; served two years in British Peace Corps in Northern Borneo; also taught local students in Singapore and Brunei; extremely active in soccer associations.

SANDY JERNBERG, page 68;
developed and team taught an enrichment summer school program on urban environment using the Mississippi River; pilot teacher for Higher Order Thinking Skills program; recognized in 1988 for developing Challengers Gifted Program; five years in classroom.

PAMELA ADAMS JOHNSON, page 29;
third generation teacher; completing her Ph.D. at the University of Iowa; 1990 Iowa Teacher of the Year; 17 year veteran; charter member of the Elementary Science Division of the Iowa Academy for Science; diehard Chicago Cubs fan.

MARY LAYCOCK, page 116;
widely published author of both books and articles; taught in Pakistan at the American School in Lahore in 1976 under sponsorship of U.S. State Department; 1989 California Educator Award; travels extensively in training teachers; proclaims her work a personal crusade concerning the teaching of math.

SISTER PAULINE LEMAIRE, page 34;
taught for many years in traditional classroom before becoming Montessori teacher; 28 year veteran; active in Montessori teacher training; father taught in Quebec, Canada; first language was French, learned English when she started school; grew up on a farm where a child "learns from observing nature and by doing."

SUSAN LLOYD, page 42;
member of first US/USSR Teacher Task Force, first such group to teach uncensored in USSR (1988); Alabama Teacher of the Year in 1989; active in Tennessee Valley Women's Conference, Church Women United, Huntsville Interfaith Peace Group; mother is a retired teacher; currently working toward certification in elementary administration.

PETER OLESEN LUND, page 85;
career has included teaching woodworking skills to blind psychiatric students at a Veterans Hospital to coaching baseball to developing drug awareness curriculum; civic profile includes 1989 Dedicated Service Award; finalist, New Hampshire Teacher of the Year.

LYNN M. MACAL, page 36;
has contributed as a writer to preschool and kindergarten student textbooks; 17 years in the classroom; member of National Reading Association; B.A., College of St. Teresa, Winona, Minnesota; M.Ed., University of Minnesota at Minneapolis.

WILMA F. MAD PLUME, page 82;
has only been teaching five years, but has received numerous awards of appreciation and for outstanding leadership, particularly for her involvement in drug and alcohol education and rehabilitation programs; 1990 State Superintendent's Achievement Award; is a member of the Montana Energy Education Council.

BART MARANTZ, page 72;
has toured with such greats as Ray Charles and Glenn Miller Orchestra; 1986 Fulbright Scholar; one of ten directors selected to visit 1989 Montreux Jazz Festival; his program has won 45 Down Beat Dee Bee Jazz Awards; former students tour with such artists as Wynton Marsalis.

DAVE MASTERMAN, page 54;
conducts workshops nationally on the teaching of science, with emphasis on use of computers in laboratory, 1988 National Science Foundation Presidential Award Winner; volunteers as mentor for elementary and junior high gifted and talented science program; professional river guide and interpreter at Grand Teton National Park.

ELAINE MATSUZAKI, page 112;
veteran of 29 years; extremely active in her church; B.A. in math from University of Hawaii; mother of five; sister and aunt are also teachers; has a deep appreciation for the mental discipline and problem-solving benefits that derive from the study of math.

GRACE HALL McENTEE, page 47;
a published author of essays, poems and stories; frequently presents workshops for other teachers on writing; works with individuals "all the time, any time" on writing; 21 years in the classroom; on Advisory Board, Brown University Teacher Education; fervent supporter of Ted Sizer's Coalition of Essential Schools.

BETTYE McLAUGHLIN, page 113;
currently sponsors the student council and the senior class; during her 34 years in the classroom, has sponsored the yearbook for 30 years, the newspaper for 22 years and the cheerleaders for 20 years; her mother's tremendous admiration for teachers influenced her career choice.

BERYL LYNNE MIRVILLE, page 66;
in the classroom for a decade; comes from a family of teachers, including both her parents; Teacher of the Year at her school 1987-88; active in the children's ministry in her church; graduate of Florida A&M University.

MARJORY MOE, page 48;
grandmother studied under Melvil Dewey at Columbia University when he was expounding his "radical" Dewey Decimal System; proudly owns grandmother's textbook from that course; participates in Speakers Corps of New Jersey Department of Education; married for 22 years; mother of three.

GEORGIE MOUTON, page 60;
her impassioned speech—in French—moved the school board to restore proposed budget cuts threatening the district-wide teaching of French and therefore the preservation of the French-Acadian culture; chaperones student groups abroad; pictured at the Acadian Village, a restored historical preservation site.

DOLLY NARANJO, page 27;
has worked throughout her 15 year career with Pueblo Native American students; developed a Pueblo opera program for children; earned degrees from College of Santa Fe and Highlands University in Las Vegas, New Mexico.

BILLY DEAN NAVE, JR., page 94;
cofounded River Valley Alternative School in 1986 after teaching seven years in self-contained class for at risk youth; discovered gift for teaching through work in New York City ghettos; 1990 Maine Teacher of the Year; one of four finalists for National Teacher of the Year.

IVAN NEAL, page 45;
credits his fourth grade teacher with inspiring him to become a teacher; active member of his church; named Teacher of the Year by both his school and district; has been teaching seven years; will complete his master's degree in July, 1990.

JEN NELSON, page 75;
honored by the Oklahoma Foundation for Excellence in Education; teacher for 15 years; has served on Oklahoma Academy for State Goals and has worked with Oklahoma Summer Arts Institute; mother and aunt were teachers; daughter, Natalie, is studying to be a teacher.

NINA PEARSON, page 42;
conducts workshops on higher level thinking skills; B.A., University of South Florida; M.A., University of Alabama, Birmingham; sponsors school newspaper; member of Gifted Underachievers; has been teaching for two years; informs parents by newsletter concerning variety of exciting minicourses available to students.

MICHELLE PECK, page 53;
including her parents, aunts, uncles, brothers and sisters, comes from a family of about 75 teachers; veteran of 13 years; sponsors Amnesty International, Junior Legislature and student summer tours of Washington, D.C.; 1989 Outstanding Educator of Jackson Hole High School.

BOBBIE SUE POOLE, page 20;
recipient of National Science Foundation Presidential Award of Excellence; 24 year veteran; active member of Nevada Team for Leading Mathematics into the 21st Century; school yearbook has twice been dedicated to both her and her husband, a teacher at the same school.

YVONNE RHEM-TITTLE, page 77;
mother of seven children and grandmother of six; sponsor of Young Astronauts Club; 18 years in the classroom; member of St. Augustine Church for 30 years; works in tutoring program for first through third graders; honored many times for community service and teaching.

CLEMONTENE W. ROUNTREE, page 33;
conducts family science programs for students and their parents; honored
many times during her 23 year career, including Presidential appointments
to two National Science Teacher Association Task Forces: Minorities in
Science and Children's Programs; also winner of Christa McAuliffe
Fellowship; husband, Dr. William Rountree, is retired educator.

MARK SAUL, page 49;
honored time and again for his leadership in mathematics competitions and
teaching, including Rickover Foundation Fellowship; National Science
Foundation Presidential Award; Certificates of Honor, Westinghouse
Science Talent Search, National Science Service; holds Ph.D. and M.A. in
mathematics from New York University and B.A. from Columbia
University.

BOB SCHROEDER, page 35;
active in environmental issues, Earth Day and recycling; received
Environmental Teacher of the Year Award from Society for Protection of
New Hampshire Forests; 1985 finalist, New Hampshire Teacher of the
Year; honored by governor as Outstanding Volunteer for tutorial work with
Stafford House of Correction; pictured at Damm Garrison House, built in
1675, at Woodman Institute.

ROBERT H. SINCLAIR, page 71;
Peace Corps volunteer in Eastern Caribbean where he taught speech and
drama and wrote plays based upon local folktales; an avid runner, former
track and cross country coach; recipient of Chancellor's/New School
Fellowship in 1988; 21 years' experience; mother taught in New York City
for over 30 years.

RICHARD SPRY, page 100;
his wife helps teach in his classroom; 1990 Tennessee Teacher of the Year;
asked that the following note be included: "Our local, state and national
teacher organizations have worked for improved salaries and working
conditions. Knowing they are there to help support us is a great comfort."

GAIL MCCREADY STAGGERS, page 118;
actively involved with interdisciplinary courses, career exploration
programs and school drama productions; 18 years in the classroom; has
received recognition from *Connecticut* magazine, University of Connecticut
and Yale New Haven Teachers Institute; also for her African-American
poetry, biography, autobiography, folktales and oral tradition.

JACQUELINE MILES STANLEY, page 28;
coordinates a 22-site pilot program designed to encourage minority middle
school students to set goals for higher education and careers in teaching;
received Governor's Award for Comprehensive Health Education Program;
is anxious to return to her classroom; pictured at Winthrop College.

DOLORES CLOUGHERTY SUVAK, page 30;
her father, Henry George Clougherty, Sr., was a long time, much-loved
educator in the community where she and her husband live; serves as
adviser for yearbook, Quill and Scroll, newspaper and cheerleaders; has
taught desegregation workshops at University of Pittsburgh; she and her
husband are active in their church.

RONALD G. SUVAK, SR., page 30;
in 1977 and 1986 he and his wife drove across the U.S. touring historical and
literary sites to gather first-hand information for teaching our heritage;
coaches football and basketball; his teams have had both undefeated and
championship seasons; also volunteers as referee for community leagues and
sponsors field trips to Washington, D.C.

CELIA VAIL, page 63;
veteran of 26 years; career includes tutoring deaf students and teaching
English as a Second Language; active in the League of Women Voters and
the planning commission for her community; has been named finalist for
Teacher of the Year of Correctional Educators of Ohio.

JORGE "COCO" VAZQUEZ, page 111;
a native of Bolivia; wide variety of teaching experiences during his 13 year
career, including rural literacy programs in South America and clinical
teaching of the severely handicapped; received Professional Best Leadership
Award from *Learning Magazine*; is a member of the Council for Exceptional
Children and Partners of the Americas.

DEBRA WEST, page 42;
actively involved in school, family, church and community;
a deaconess in her church, participates in nursing home visitation program;
also volunteers in camp for underprivileged youth; completed
undergraduate degree and continues toward graduate degree while raising
five children; elder sister is a teacher, also.

MAC WESTMORELAND, page 58;
Steering Committee, State Teachers Forum; has conducted staff
development ropes course for teachers and staff; four years as assistant
principal but chose to go back to the classroom; proud father and husband
who describes his wife as "probably the best kindergarten teacher in the
world."

LYNN A. WILHELM, page 108;
developed outdoor education and gardening/ecological site at her school;
students donate all garden produce to local food pantry and nursing homes;
has taught gardening skills to mentally handicapped; developed network of
community resource experts who work with her classes; 1990 Indiana
Teacher of the Year finalist.

VIRGIL WILKINS, page 83;
more than three-quarters of a million dollars have been poured into the
economy of his community through his students' agricultural enterprises;
student once sold a ham for $11,970, a world record price at that time;
serves as mayor of his community; 27 year veteran.

EDWARD J. WONG, page 41;
served on Teacher Advisory Committee to the State Superintendent of
Education in 1989; developed unique course in Mississippi River history;
1987 Mississippi Teacher of the Year; volunteers with American Heart
Association, Special Olympics, Red Cross and Mayor's Commission on
Drug Awareness; pictured at Civil War memorial site near Vicksburg.

VERLEETA WOOTEN, page 80;
sponsors the African-American Club at West Seattle High School; teacher
for 19 years; has been recognized for Outstanding Educational Service by
Seattle University Black Student Union; has coached numerous extra-
curricular activities; is completing graduate work at Western Washington
University.

If you are interested in becoming a teacher, contact:

American Association of Colleges of Teacher Education
AACTE/ERIC Clearinghouse on Teacher Education
One Dupont Circle, Suite 610
Washington, D.C. 20036
(202) 293-2450

or contact:

Recruiting New Teachers, Inc.
6 Standish Street
Cambridge, Massachusetts 02138
1-800-45-TEACH

For more information about the
I AM A TEACHER project, contact:

Corporation for Education
P.O. Box 141196
Dallas, Texas 75214
(214) 824-3485